A
Composition
Handbook

/87

A Composition Handbook

THIRD EDITION

William E. Merriss
EMERITUS
Greenwich Country Day School

and

David H. Griswold

Greenwich Country Day School

Longman
New York & London

A Composition Handbook

Copyright © 1969, 1976, 1985 by Longman

Copyright © 1965 by W. E. Merriss and D. H. Griswold

Longman, 10 Bank Street, White Plains, N.Y. 10606

Associated companies:
Longman Group Ltd., London
Longman Cheshire Pty., Melbourne
Longman Paul Pty., Auckland
Copp Clark Pitman, Toronto

ISBN 0-88334-186-7

8 9 10-MA-9594

PREFACE TO THE THIRD EDITION

When *A Composition Handbook* first appeared in print almost twenty years ago, the authors little suspected that it would be so soundly supported by teachers and students throughout the United States. For such support and confidence, this brief word of thanks to all who have used and benefited from the *Handbook*.

This third edition maintains the basic design of the previous editions. However, a number of changes have been made — for the better, we think. First, the rule numbers have been simplified to eliminate numerical subscripts. Second, recent changes in punctuation have been included (e.g., no period after Postal Service abbreviations of states like MA, CT, and CA). Third, the exercises have been extensively revised and expanded to include more sentences and more challenging problems. Finally, old rules have been revised and new ones included to deal with the most recent coinage by students (e.g., *like when*).

The authors are grateful to Thomas P. Beal, Jr., for his thoughtful suggestions in this edition. Special thanks go to Anne Griswold for her expert copyediting, her professional proofreading, and her careful indexing.

William E. Merriss
David H. Griswold

TO THE TEACHER

PLEASE READ THE FOLLOWING
BEFORE YOU USE THIS BOOK

This book is designed:
- To establish a *uniform* system for the correction of compositions. It can be used effectively beginning at the seventh grade.
- To make clear to students *exactly* what their errors are.
- To help students *correct* these errors in such a way that they will learn from their mistakes.
- To encourage the use of *concrete, graphic* language.
- To help students improve their sentences, their paragraphs, and their overall compositions *systematically*.
- To make clear to students how to organize and develop their compositions by effective *outlining*.
- To be a handy reference book in the usage of the language.

This book is *NOT* designed:
- To be an instructional, comprehensive grammar book.
- To be a work manual or a drill book.
- To turn all students into creative writers.
- To be a spelling book.
- To give a philological background of language.

A Composition Handbook is, at the very least, just that. If it does turn out to be convenient as an occasional grammar book, so much the better, but we wish to emphasize that the primary objective in putting together and revising the *Handbook* is to create a uniform method for the correcting of compositions.

At the same time, with the exception of *Sp.* (spelling), we have done away with all idiosyncratic correction symbols. Having used this book for almost twenty years, we feel confident that it has made the burden of composition correction easier, speedier, and more effective for student and teacher alike.

Such adjectives are not justified, however, unless this book is used precisely and conscientiously. Above all, it is a tool designed to be useful and to be used by both teacher and students.

In this connection, please read carefully the section immediately following, which recommends an effective method for the practical use of the *Handbook.*

HOW TO USE THIS BOOK

A Composition Handbook can be used profitably in grade seven on up through high school. Naturally, seventh graders are not expected to know all the rules found in this book, but they certainly may be held responsible for as many as twenty or thirty.

With this in mind, we have put the rules most frequently broken at the beginning of each chapter. We then suggest to our seventh grade teachers that they decide what rules the students are responsible for and mark their compositions with that in mind. The same procedures will, of course, be followed by eighth grade teachers and so on up through all grades.

STEP 1: INSTRUCTION BEFORE WRITING THE COMPOSITION

Before students write their compositions, the *Handbook* can be used profitably to instruct them in the way to write a proper outline (see Appendix 8) or the mechanics of paragraphing (see Chapters 23 and 24).

Furthermore, if teachers feel that certain mechanical devices need to be emphasized (the comma, for example), they can go over the appropriate chapter before assigning the topic. An effective device is to stress that penalty points in that area will be increased for that particular composition, and that students should proofread for violations of the rules stressed before handing their work in.

STEP 2: TEACHER'S CORRECTIONS (See model on facing page.)

Use the Abbreviated Correction Sheet, printed in the front of the Teacher's Guide.

Each teacher will have an Abbreviated Correction Sheet, usually pasted on the back of a manila folder.

We have given JRW an 85 at the top of his composition, and that might be a fair grade for a seventh grader if the composition were free of mechanical errors. Because we do not wish to stress mechanics at the expense of creativity, we always start off with what we judge is the correct grade based on *originality, organization,* and *style.*

Then we subtract from that original grade penalties outlined below, a copy of which each student should have.

Suggested penalties (to be used at the discretion of the teacher):
- 5 off for each Sentence Error
- 3 off for misspellings of: *two, too, to; all right; a lot* (See 13X)
- 2 off for lazy words such as: *go, went, come, came, lots of,* etc.
- 1 off for abusage and usage stressed in class (See Chaps. 13 and 14)
- 1 off for ordinary misspellings
- 1 off for punctuation stressed in class
- 1 off for awkwardness and rewrites
- 1 off for choice of words, sentence variety, lack of parallelism, wordiness, repetition, etc.

MODEL OF COMPOSITION AND TEACHER'S CORRECTIONS

85
- 5 SE
- 3 too
- 1 gram
- 2 punct
———
74

4/7/83

Ghost Story

It was a dark night, Emma
was alone in the house reading
a good book. The ticking of the
clock and the sound of the wind
was lonesome and eerie.

Suddenly Emma heard a
subdued "Click" from the kitchen,
almost to quiet to be perceived.
Emma jumped.

"My god," she thought. "what
was that?"

Emma slowly inched her
way to the door leading to the kitchen. She heard a faint humming.
Emma sighed with relief when
she realized the noises were
emanating from her automatic
dishwasher.

1A
13 G
11C
13X
1F
24B

TO THE STUDENT *AND* THE TEACHER

STEP 3: STUDENT'S CORRECTIONS: INSTRUCTIONS

Write corrections in the order they occur on your paper.
Even if you have identical mistakes on your paper, you must complete all the required steps for each violation.

(See model on pages xii and xiii.)

For Corrections Other Than Sentence Errors (Rules in Chap. 1)
1. Write the number of the rule violation in the left-hand margin.
2. Write out the rule completely.
3. Skip a line.
4. Write your sentence correcting your mistake. Do not write out the entire sentence: just four or five words on either side.
5. Underline or circle where your mistake was located.

Spelling Errors
1. For ordinary misspellings, write the word correctly five times.
2. For 13X rule, write the word correctly *in context* ten times (e.g., "*too* hot," "*their* books," etc.)

Penmanship Errors
Write the word legibly five times.

Sentence Errors (Rules in Chap. 1)
1. Write the number of the rule violation in the left-hand margin.
2. Write out the rule completely.
3. Skip a line.
4. Write out sentence(s) correctly, underlining or circling where your mistake was located.
   NOTE: With Sentence Errors, you must write out the *entire* sentence or sentences.
5. Skip a line.
6. Do sentences 1-5 of the exercise immediately following the rule.

    (Continued on next page.)

Sentence Errors (continued)

If you have a second Sentence Error of the same rule, do sentences 6-10 of the same exercise.

If you have a third Sentence Error of the same rule, just do steps 1-4 above.

More Than One Mistake in a Sentence

If you have more than one mistake in a sentence, you must write all the rules you have violated, but you need write the corrected sentence only once.

(Model of student's corrections on next two pages)

MODEL OF STUDENT'S CORRECTIONS

JRW   *Composition Corrections*

1A Do not join two independent clauses with only a comma between them.

13 G Avoid the lazy use of <u>good</u> and <u>bad</u>.

<u>Sentence</u>: It was a dark night⊙ Emma was alone in the house reading a <u>fascinating</u> book.

<u>Exercise</u> 1A

1. Waldo enjoys playing basketball⊙ His older brother prefers wrestling.

2. After lunch, the couple strolled down the avenue⊙ Then they took a bus to the ball game.

3. Most teachers enjoy teaching⊙ Most students do not enjoy studying.

4. Two cars were damaged in the accident⊙ Luckily no one was hurt.

MODEL OF STUDENT'S CORRECTIONS

5. The climb to the top of the mountain was difficult⊙ The canoe trip was more enjoyable.

'C Compound subjects take a plural verb.

Sentence: The ticking ... and the sound ... were lonesome ....

?X too quiet   too quiet
too quiet   too quiet
too quiet   too quiet
too quiet   too quiet
too quiet   too quiet

'F Capitalize references to diety.
"My God," she thought.

+B Syllabify the last word in a line correctly. kitch-en

STEP 4: CORRECTIONS CORRECTED

Because JRW has done a conscientious job in the way he has done his corrections, we have returned all his points. We have found that the majority of students are eager to set to work immediately on their corrections and that such eagerness is beneficial because the students are doing their corrections while the composition is fresh in their minds.

We would like to stress, however, that flexibility is required. It is silly to be overly mathematical, overly pedantic in the correction of any kind of writing. What we are primarily concerned with is lucidity, precision, and above all, the avoidance of the lazy, lackluster word or verbal device.

To repeat, this book is only a tool—a tool, however, that is a useful guide not only for students but also for new, inexperienced teachers—and the head of the department. The latter has some idea as to how the teaching of composition is going and knows, too, that there is a kind of uniformity in the department.

STEP 5: FURTHER DRILL

If the student is having difficulty in a particular area after doing the corrections, the teacher may decide that further drill is needed.

For this purpose, exercises have been included at the end of many rules to help students strengthen their grasp of weak areas.

USE IN REVIEW

Many of the exercises have been found to be useful for a quick review by advanced students and by those taking College Boards.

Chapters 17-22 and their exercises are especially recommended for such review.

Table of Contents

EFFECTIVE WORD CHOICE

Sentence Errors

1 **Definition of a SENTENCE:** *A SENTENCE is a group of words (generally containing a subject and a verb) that expresses a complete thought.*

Students must learn what a sentence is and learn how it is to be punctuated before it can be said that they know how to write.

There are two types of *Sentence Errors:*
        RUN-ON SENTENCES and
        SENTENCE FRAGMENTS
1. Two independent clauses with no punctuation or with only a comma separating them is called a *RUN-ON SENTENCE.* (See 1A, 1B, and 1C.)
2. A group of words that does *not* express a complete thought is a *SENTENCE FRAGMENT.* (See 1D, 1E, and 1F.)

Examples of subordinate clauses that are sentence fragments:

SENTENCE   My father loves me. *Because I have always done what he*
ERROR   *wanted.*

COMPLETED My father loves me because I have always done what he
SENTENCE   wanted.

COMPLETED My father loves me. I have always done what he wanted.
SENTENCES

BEWARE PARTICULARLY OF SENTENCE ERRORS IN QUOTATIONS.

SENTENCE   *"When I saw the moon rising," she said.* "It was in the
ERROR   east."

COMPLETED "When I saw the moon rising," she said, "it was in the
SENTENCE   east."

COMPLETED "I saw the moon rising," she said. "It pulled itself
SENTENCES slowly up the horizon."

1

Sentence Errors

RUN-ON SENTENCES

1 A DO NOT JOIN TWO INDEPENDENT CLAUSES WITH ONLY A COMMA BETWEEN THEM.

TO CORRECT: USE A PERIOD INSTEAD OF THE COMMA OR USE THE PROPER SUBORDINATION OR COORDINATION.

COMMENT: Two independent clauses with only a comma between them is called a COMMA SPLICE or a RUN-ON SENTENCE.

SENTENCE ERROR   I never knew my Uncle Bill, he died when I was young.

CORRECTED SENTENCES   I never knew my Uncle Bill. He died when I was young.

Because my Uncle Bill died when I was young, I never knew him.

SENTENCE ERROR   In Latin we are studying the subjunctive mood, so far no one understands it.

CORRECTED SENTENCES   In Latin we are studying the subjunctive mood. So far, no one understands it.

Although we are now studying the subjunctive mood in Latin, no one, so far, understands it.

Sentence Errors

1 A DIRECTIONS: Rewrite the following sentences and correct the
sentence errors.

Part I

1. Waldo enjoys playing basketball, his older brother prefers
   wrestling.

2. After lunch, the couple strolled down the avenue, then they took a
   bus to the ball game.

3. Most teachers enjoy teaching, most students do not enjoy studying.

4. Two cars were damaged in the accident, luckily no one was hurt.

5. The climb to the top of the mountain was difficult, the canoe trip was
   more enjoyable.

Part II

6. At the start of the season, the coach knew little about soccer, at the
   end of the season, he had gained experience.

7. Willie made many sentence errors in the sixth grade, in the ninth
   grade, he still makes the same mistakes.

8. After the doctor arrived, she checked the patient, then she asked
   for some boiling water.

9. When we looked at the painting, we began to laugh, it looked like
   finger painting.

10. Enoch did not have enough money, of course, he could not buy the
    book he wanted.

Sentence Errors

1 B **DO NOT MAKE SENTENCE ERRORS WHEN USING QUOTATION MARKS.**

TO CORRECT: USE A PERIOD OR THE CORRECT PUNCTUATION BETWEEN THE SENTENCES.

SENTENCE ERROR	"Buy a new hat," she said, "it will make you feel better."
CORRECTED SENTENCE	"Buy a new hat," she said. "It will make you feel better."
SENTENCE ERROR	"Whom did you meet in Dublin," he asked, "was it your nephew?"
CORRECTED SENTENCE	"Whom did you meet in Dublin?" he asked. "Was it your nephew?"
SENTENCE ERROR	"The night was dark, I was in the house alone," said Kim.
CORRECTED SENTENCE	"The night was dark. I was in the house alone," said Kim.

1 **B**

Sentence Errors

B   DIRECTIONS: Rewrite the following sentences and correct the
sentence errors.

Part I

1.   "I'm tired," complained the boy, "can't we go home now?"

2.   "The race is over," he said breathing heavily, "did I win?"

3.   "I asked you to meet me at the hotel," said the girl, "you
never showed up."

4.   "Then join the Marines," said the angry wife, "see if I care."

5.   "Pass me the ball!" yelled Corey, "I'm in the clear!"

Part II

6.   "Here is your money back," said the clerk, "we hope you are
satisfied."

7.   "You have helped with the lawn," my father said, "now go
help your mother in the kitchen."

8.   "Is that you, Willie, are you in the kitchen?" asked Mother.

9.   "I have studied the book closely," the teacher remarked, "I
wish you would do the same."

10.   "What is your name?" the police officer asked, "where do
you live?"

Sentence Errors

RUN-ON SENTENCES

1 c **DO NOT CARELESSLY JOIN TWO INDEPENDENT CLAUSES WITH NO PUNCTUATION BETWEEN THEM.**

TO CORRECT: USE A PERIOD (NOT A COMMA) BETWEEN THE TWO CLAUSES, OR THE CORRECT SUBORDINATION.

COMMENT: Two independent clauses with no punctuation between them is also called a RUN-ON SENTENCE (as in Rule 1A).

SENTENCE ERROR: Sloan stepped into his car he turned the key to the ignition.

CORRECTED SENTENCES: Sloan stepped into his car. He turned the key to the ignition.

When Sloan stepped into his car, he turned the key to the ignition.

SENTENCE ERROR: The student tried to find the word in the dictionary he searched for a minute and then gave up.

CORRECTED SENTENCES: The student tried to find the word in the dictionary. He searched for a minute and then gave up.

1 **c**

Sentence Errors

EXERCISE 1C

DIRECTIONS: Rewrite the following sentences using periods where
they belong, or the correct subordination.

Part I

1. The day was very hot the radio predicted tornadoes.

2. A porpoise likes to play in the water it is a friendly animal.

3. Writing compositions can be fun writing corrections is a bore.

4. Richard slept a sound sleep his wife tossed and turned.

5. Optimism is hoping for the best to happen most Americans
    are optimistic.

Part II

6. Good writing is a sign of good training poor writing is a sign
    of sloppiness.

7. Stocks can be risky bonds are generally a safer investment.

8. Walter won the prize for scholarship Phyllis won the attend-
    ance award.

9. Walking is good exercise jogging is even more strenuous.

10. Arithmetic is a basic skill algebra is more difficult.

Sentence Errors

CLAUSE FRAGMENTS

1 D DO NOT WRITE A SUBORDINATE CLAUSE AS A COMPLETE SENTENCE.

TO CORRECT: *ADD AN INDEPENDENT CLAUSE* BEFORE *OR* AFTER *THE SUBORDINATE CLAUSE.*

SENTENCE ERROR
When the lacrosse team returned from Baltimore.

COMPLETED SENTENCE
When the lacrosse team returned from Baltimore, *we gave them a cheer.*

SENTENCE ERROR
The Latin teacher gave us a vocabulary book. Which he insisted would be useful.

COMPLETED SENTENCE
The Latin teacher gave us a vocabulary book, *which he insisted would be useful.*

SENTENCE ERROR
Why our orange juice squeezer was useful in preparing breakfast.

COMPLETED SENTENCE
Mary explained why our orange juice squeezer was useful in preparing breakfast.

1 **D**

Sentence Errors

EXERCISE 1D

D DIRECTIONS: Rewrite the following sentence fragments so that they express a complete thought. Join any fragmented clauses standing alone to an original independent clause.

Part I

1. When the students complained of their arduous homework assignments in English.

2. Where the Mississippi River joins the muddy Missouri River north of St. Louis.

3. Which impressed nearly all of the students.

4. After the team members had taken their showers, dressed, and left the gym.

5. That he did not choose to run for dog catcher.

Part II

6. How the disciplined English regulars eventually lost to the tattered colonial troops in the American Revolution.

7. When an eighth grade boy falls desperately in love with a ninth grade girl.

8. After the captain of the football team had lost his shoulder pads and helmet.

9. While the band played and the dancers did the bump.

10. Because he was intelligent, quick-witted, and wealthy.

EX **D** **1**

Sentence Errors

DO NOT WRITE PREPOSITIONAL OR VERBAL PHRASES AS COMPLETE SENTENCES.

TO CORRECT JOIN THE PHRASE TO AN INDEPENDENT CLAUSE AND PUNCTUATE CORRECTLY.

SENTENCE ERROR   I saw him sink beneath the waves. Finally giving up all hope. (Participle phrase)

COMPLETED SENTENCE   I saw him, finally giving up all hope, sink beneath the waves.

SENTENCE ERROR   Soon the football team began to regain confidence. First in their line play and later in their pass attack. (Prepositional phrases)

COMPLETED SENTENCE   Soon the football team began to regain confidence, first in their line play and later in their pass attack.

SENTENCE ERROR   "He will want to see his old friends," Bill said. "To borrow money from them." (Infinitive phrase)

COMPLETED SENTENCE   "He will want to see his old friends," Bill said, "to borrow money from them."

Sentence Errors

E   DIRECTIONS: Rewrite the following sentence fragments so that they
              express a complete thought.

Part I

1.   After taking in the sea and sand. He returned to work.

2.   The detective spotted the criminal. Walking into the
      department store.

3.   At the beginning of the game. The coach sent in his best
      players.

4.   Wilmer put away a little money every week. To buy his wife a
      birthday present.

5.   While smoking a long, black Havana cigar. The cowboy
      calmly shot down five bandits and one old lady.

Part II

6.   Slowly stepping into the living room. He saw that he was not
      alone.

7.   In the middle of the night after a shocking experience. Lady
      Macbeth decided to go for a stroll in the castle.

8.   To find the church you are looking for. Go down three
      blocks and turn left.

9.   "On the top shelf in the kitchen," my wife explained. "You
      will see a large, brown paper bag."

10.   "Help me," the sailor asked. "To bring the ship safely to
      shore."

Sentence Errors

WORD FRAGMENTS

1 F DO NOT WRITE WORD FRAGMENTS AS COMPLETE SENTENCES.

TO CORRECT: JOIN THE WORD FRAGMENTS TO THE INDEPENDENT CLAUSE AND PUNCTUATE CORRECTLY.

COMMENT: Be particularly careful of word groups beginning with *and, for example, for instance, first, especially, also, such as,* and others. Be careful, too, with *appositive elements.* (See 2H.)

SENTENCE ERROR In the museum we saw many old cars. Such as Edsels, Maxwells, and LaSalles.

COMPLETED SENTENCE In the museum we saw many old cars such as Edsels, Maxwells, and LaSalles.

SENTENCE ERROR "I had an idea for making money," he said. "An idea that was brilliant." (Appositive element)

COMPLETED SENTENCE "I had an idea for making money," he said, "an idea that was brilliant."

SENTENCE ERROR The football coach had many friends. Became a Democrat and was elected to the state senate.

COMPLETED SENTENCE The football coach had many friends, became a Democrat, and was elected to the state senate.

SENTENCE ERROR He left New York. And took the plans with him.

COMPLETED SENTENCE He left New York and took the plans with him.

1 F

Sentence Errors

EXERCISE 1F

F   DIRECTIONS: Rewrite the following sentence fragments so that they express a complete thought.

Part I

1.   Tara purchased many cheap items. Especially paper clips and rubber bands.

2.   He was a superb rider. A crack shot with a pistol, and a clever military strategist.

3.   "Phoebe is a girl of great talent," said the teacher. "Talent that she unfortunately does not use."

4.   Our family likes skiing in Vermont. And sailing on Long Island Sound.

5.   "You are too fat," said the doctor. "Too lazy,. and too slovenly."

Part II

6.   He disliked the Japanese dinner. A meal consisting of raw fish, octopus, and lotus leaves.

7.   "I cannot agree with your ideas," said the judge. "Your methods, or your approach."

8.   "Fido came home," said Eloise. "His collar missing and his spirit broken."

9.   Oscar respected his teacher. But did not want to become a teacher himself.

10.   He was fond of snakes. Such as cobras, rattlers, and asps.

Sentence Errors

SEMICOLON

1 G   DO NOT USE A COMMA BETWEEN INDEPENDENT CLAUSES JOINED BY CONJUNCTIVE ADVERBS OR TRANSITIONAL EXPRESSIONS.

TO CORRECT: USE A PERIOD (OR SEMICOLON) FOR THE COMMA.

Some conjunctive adverbs:
*also, anyhow, besides, conse-
quently, furthermore, however,
indeed, instead, moreover,
meanwhile, nevertheless,
otherwise, still, then, therefore,
too* (meaning *also*), and
sometimes *so* and *yet*.

Some transitional expressions:
*for example, in fact, on the
contrary, on the other hand,
that is, first, second, for instance, as a result, at this time.*

NOTE: *THE INDISCRIMINATE USE OF SEMICOLONS (TO PLAY IT SAFE) WILL BE CONSIDERED A SENTENCE ERROR.*

COMMENT #1:   The semicolon always *precedes* the connective.

COMMENT #2:   Although *so* is included in the list, avoid its use altogether to mean *therefore, as a result.* Instead, use subordination. For incorrect use of *so,* see 13S.

AVOID   She was popular; so she was invited to many parties.

CORRECTED   Because she was popular, she was invited to many
SENTENCE   parties.

(Continued on next page.)

Sentence Errors

EXAMPLES

SENTENCE   We graciously thanked our hostess, then we realized it
ERROR   was the maid.

CORRECTED   We graciously thanked our hostess; then we realized it
SENTENCE   was the maid.

SENTENCE   It was a pleasant holiday, first we had a picnic lunch,
ERROR   and then we bowled.

CORRECTED   It was a pleasant holiday. First we had a picnic lunch,
SENTENCES   and then we bowled.

SENTENCE   Martha enjoyed compliments, however, she felt uncom-
ERROR   fortable when they became insincere.

CORRECTED   Martha enjoyed compliments. However, she felt uncom-
SENTENCES   fortable when they became insincere.

SENTENCE   Mr. Palmer encouraged his students, that is, he gave
ERROR   them big bonuses.

CORRECTED   **Mr. Palmer encouraged his students; that is, he gave**
SENTENCE   them big bonuses.

(Exercise on next page.)

1 G

Sentence Errors

1 G DIRECTIONS: Rewrite the following sentences using periods or
semicolons to correct the sentence errors.
(Correct misused semicolons.)

Part I

1. Ken was a poor quarterback, for example, he lost at least seven
    yards on every play.

2. No one doubted the convict's guilt, nevertheless, he was
    reprieved.

3. The dessert was spoiled, thus; nearly everyone became ill.

4. Bowling is good for one's health, indeed, one should
    try to bowl at least once a week.

5. The fair was exciting, first we saw the fat lady, and then we
    ate lunch.

Part II

6. Snow covered the treacherous mountain, still we decided to
    climb to the top.

7. The dinner was ready at last, finally the campers sat down to
    eat.

8. The soldier was handsome, however, he was cowardly.

9. The man put a banana in each ear, as a result, he could not
    hear.

10. Honesty is important to one's self-respect, moreover;
    it is essential in the conduct of human affairs.

Sentence Errors

1 **REVIEW**   This exercise includes all violations of the
EXERCISE: sentence error rules.

DIRECTIONS: Rewrite the following sentences to correct the
sentence errors. Join fragmented clauses or phrases
standing alone to an original independent clause.

1.   He is very weak, in fact, he cannot get out of bed.

2.   The robber cantered out of town, meanwhile, a posse was being formed.

3.   So that a student can learn to write clear, simple, and effective prose.

4.   A month afterward, since his uncle had insisted upon a June wedding at St. Patrick's.

5.   "I bought a new hat," said the man. "One that will please you."

6.   Miss Petit had always liked ancient history. Especially the story of the Hittites.

7.   "I do not like," said the teacher. "Either your attitude or your work."

8.   "Golfing was a healthy pastime," said the headmaster. "Until golf carts were invented."

9.   "Of course I will not lend you the money," stormed the father, "on the contrary, I am disowning you."

10.   He suffered a twisted ankle, nevertheless, he won the race.

(Continued on next page.)

REV EX **1**

Sentence Errors

11.   Cara could not run at all. For she had blisters on her toes.

12.   I never knew why the stars were so bright. Until I studied a book on astronomy.

13.   He knew where he was going, he knew how to reach his goals.

14.   Wilma bought a new pair of sunglasses. To protect her eyes from the sun.

15.   The mailman walked to the corner then he turned down Main Street.

16.   When Howard was in Spain last summer.

17.   He gained his experience with pistols. First in the army and later with the FBI.

18.   Seeing that it was impossible to start the car.

19.   He was not rich, in fact; he did not have a penny to his name.

20.   After the red sun had sunk slowly beneath the horizon.

Commas

COORDINATING CONJUNCTIONS

2 A

USE A COMMA BETWEEN INDEPENDENT CLAUSES JOINED BY THE COORDINATING CONJUNCTIONS *AND, BUT, OR, NOR, FOR* (AND SOMETIMES *SO* AND *YET*).

PATTERN:

Coordinating
conjunctions
and
but
Independent clause, *or* independent clause
nor
for

EXAMPLES: We arrived at the school early, *and* there we found many of our classmates.

It snowed all night, *but* the school was open bright and early the next morning.

COMMENT #1: *And* and *but* are coordinating conjunctions and, as such, should rarely be used to begin a sentence.

COMMENT #2: Some authorities consider *yet* and *so* coordinating conjunctions. The decision here must lie with the instructor.

A 2

Commas

INTRODUCTORY ELEMENTS

2 B   **USE A COMMA AFTER AN ADVERB CLAUSE THAT INTRODUCES AN INDEPENDENT CLAUSE.**

EXAMPLES: *Because the English teacher was in a good humor,* the class tended to take advantage of him.

If a child works diligently, he will be rewarded.

2 C   **USE A COMMA AFTER LONG INTRODUCTORY PHRASES OR A SERIES OF PHRASES THAT INTRODUCE INDEPENDENT CLAUSES.**

EXAMPLE OF LONG INTRODUCTORY PHRASE:
Of all the new buildings erected here on the campus, the dining hall is the most striking.

EXAMPLE OF INTRODUCTORY SERIES OF PREPOSITIONAL PHRASES:
At the corner of Main Street, the traffic officer took the stand.

EXAMPLES OF INTRODUCTORY VERBAL PHRASES:

Before hitting the ball, Bill gripped the bat tightly. *(Gerund phrase)*

Roaring down Locust Avenue, the car took a quick turn and disappeared into the night. *(Participle phrase)*

To win the prize, most of the students were quite willing to do extra work. *(Infinitive phrase)*

2   **B**
C

20

Commas

TRANSITIONAL EXPRESSIONS/INTERJECTIONS

D USE A COMMA AFTER (1) INTRODUCTORY TRANSITIONAL EXPRESSIONS AND (2) MILD INTERJECTIONS: *YES, NO,* OR A SIMILAR RESPONSE.

Some introductory expressions:

accordingly	*furthermore*
also	*in fact*
as a result	*moreover*
at last	*nevertheless*
at this time	*on the other hand*
consequently	*otherwise*
finally	*second*
first	*similarly*
for example	*then*
for instance	*therefore*

EXAMPLE OF INTRODUCTORY TRANSITIONAL EXPRESSION:

Furthermore, the track team was not expected to win.

Some mild interjections:

oh	*all right*
no	*certainly*
well	*unfortunately*
why	*yes*

EXAMPLES OF INTERJECTIONS:

Well, what do you want to do about it?

All right, you come with me.

21   **D 2**

Commas

IN A SERIES

2 E USE COMMAS TO SEPARATE WORDS, PHRASES, AND SUBORDINATE AND INDEPENDENT CLAUSES IN A SERIES.

COMMENT: A comma must be placed between each item in the series.

EXAMPLES OF WORDS IN A SERIES:

His greeting to the students was *warm, friendly,* and *sincere.* (Adjectives in a series)

She wrote *courteously, sincerely,* and *eloquently.* (Adverbs in a series)

We bought *pencils, paper,* and *banners.* (Nouns in a series)

They all disliked the *grouchy, irascible, cynical* English teacher. (Coordinate adjectives modifying the same noun)

COMMENT: There is no comma between *English* and *teacher*. *English,* like *grouchy* and *irascible,* is an adjective modifying *teacher,* but it is not coordinate; that it, it cannot change place with either of the other two adjectives. We cannot say *grouchy, English, irascible teacher. English teacher* is an adjective-noun combination, but has the force of a single noun. It should be stressed that there is never a comma between the last adjective in a series and the noun it modifies. For this reason, then, there will be no comma after *cynical* since it modifies the noun *English teacher.*

Commas

EXAMPLE OF PREPOSITIONAL PHRASES IN A SERIES:

The headmaster stomped *down the hall, into the study hall,* and *up onto the platform.*

EXAMPLE OF SUBORDINATE CLAUSES IN A SERIES:

The students felt *that the English teacher was kind, that he was generous,* and *that he was trying too hard to be popular.*

EXAMPLE OF INDEPENDENT CLAUSES IN A SERIES:

Ellen was lovely, she was generous, and *she was thoroughly unprincipled.*

E 2

Commas

EXERCISE   This exercise includes comma usage for rules 2A-2E.

DIRECTIONS: Copy the sentences below and insert the necessary commas.

1.   For lunch the pupils were served hot dogs milk potato chips and ice cream.

2.   After the students had received their grades they ranted grumbled raved and shouted.

3.   The right end scampered to the ten-yard line turned to his right waited for the pass and dropped the ball.

4.   The referee was tough and ugly but he was fair.

5.   The school bus stopped near the gymnasium and forty students poured out.

6.   At the end of the Princeton game the spectators left quickly quietly and soberly.

7.   Well as she said yesterday she will come to your party but she cannot stay late.

8.   In the middle of the night Mr. Pothers padded down to the kitchen and ate a pickle some salami and a banana.

9.   Mr. Withers was handsome he was gentlemanly and he was generous.

10.   As she reached the corner of the street Norma saw a car accelerate go through a red light and disappear around the block.

Commas

ADDRESSES, DATES, GEOGRAPHY

**2 F   USE COMMAS TO SEPARATE EACH ELEMENT IN DATES AND
ADDRESSES, AND TO SEPARATE THE PARTS OF
GEOGRAPHIC NAMES.**

EXAMPLE OF DATE:

On *May 1, 1946,* there was an unusually fine gathering at Union Square.
(Note especially the comma after *1946.*)

EXAMPLE OF ADDRESS:

Send my mail to *Old Church Road, Greenwich, Connecticut* 06830.
(No comma between state and zip code)

EXAMPLE OF DATE, ADDRESS, GEOGRAPHY:

On *Saturday, July 14, 1914,* a son was born to *Mr. and Mrs. Jones,
17 West Sylvan Road, East Norwalk, Connecticut* 06855.

COMMENT: No comma separates *May 1, July 14,* or *17 West Sylvan
Road.* Convention has decreed that the day of the
month and the street and its number be considered a
single unit.

NOTE: When addressing a letter, use a comma before *Jr., Sr.,
M.D.,* and other similar designations.

EXAMPLES: William Parsons, M.D.
George Smith, Esq.

F 2

Commas

DIRECT ADDRESS

2 G   USE COMMAS TO SET OFF WORDS IN DIRECT ADDRESS.

EXAMPLES: *Mary,* bring me the apple.

Come here, *Richard,* and show me your homework.

COMMENT: For Latin scholars, the noun in direct address would be
in the vocative case in Latin.

Commas

APPOSITIVES

2 H **USE COMMAS TO SET OFF APPOSITIVES (AND THEIR MODIFIERS).**

COMMENT #1: An *appositive* is a noun or noun phrase that follows a noun or pronoun and generally gives the reader additional information.

EXAMPLES: The headmaster, *an unusually fine golfer,* liked to play at St. Andrews at the beginning of the school year.

He was introduced to his roommates, *Drummle and Startop.*

An ardent baseball fan, Mindy went to the Red Sox games every chance she could.

COMMENT #2: Negative appositives (sometimes called contrasting elements) are also set off by commas.

EXAMPLE: Dogs, *not cats,* have become a plague in many towns of this state.

NOTE: Commas must be placed on *both* sides of an appositive.

WRONG: Ted Turner's boat, the *Courageous* is slipping into the lead.

RIGHT: Ted Turner's boat, the *Courageous,* is slipping into the lead.

H 2

Commas

PARENTHETICAL EXPRESSIONS

2 I   USE COMMAS TO SET OFF PARENTHETICAL EXPRESSIONS AND CONJUNCTIVE ADVERBS.

Some parenthetical expressions:
I believe (think, know, hope, etc.), I am sure, on the other hand, after all, by the way, of course, in my opinion, for example, in the first place, that is.

Some conjunctive adverbs:
however, furthermore, nevertheless, then, moreover, and *too* (meaning *also*)
(See also 1G.)

EXAMPLE OF PARENTHETICAL PHRASE:
The boys, *by the way,* will certainly defeat the girls in field hockey.

EXAMPLE OF CONJUNCTIVE ADVERB:
The girls, *however,* will defeat the boys in the spelling bee.

COMMENT #1:   When a clause is used parenthetically, it, too, will be set off by commas.

EXAMPLE: The Dean of Studies, *if he does come,* will have only pleasant words to say to you.

COMMENT #2:   When adjectives follow nouns, set them off by commas.

EXAMPLE: Cindy, *always bright and happy,* was something of a bore to her classmates.

Commas

EXERCISE This exercise includes comma usage for rules 2A-2I.

DIRECTIONS: Copy the sentences below and insert commas where needed.

1. After it had reached the top of the hill the car stalled and its engine dropped out.

2. Of course we know that he is handsome that he is honest and that he is talented.

3. John Phrump the captain of the track team left his house ran to the corner of Main and Elm and missed the bus.

4. Andrea bring me that letter addressed to the President 1400 Pennsylvania Avenue Washington D.C. 20500.

5. Moreover Mr. Smith it was your children not your guinea pigs who ate my petunias.

6. It was either on May 4 1967 or December 6 1967 that father awoke in the middle of the night put on his bathrobe went outside and left his family forever.

7. Incidentally Jacob Fritz the distinguished Austrian composer will be invited to cook eggs corn and lobsters for the clam-bake.

8. No after the football was thrown it wobbled in the air and struck Jones not Carleton on his right ear.

9. On the wall nearest the kitchen she hung pictures of Nixon Reagan and herself.

10. Bill to his credit passed all his exams and then he passed out.

Commas

NONRESTRICTIVE CLAUSES AND PHRASES

2 J   **USE COMMAS TO SET OFF NONRESTRICTIVE ADJECTIVE CLAUSES AND PHRASES.**

COMMENT ON RESTRICTIVE CLAUSES AND PHRASES:
> You must learn to distinguish between nonrestrictive and restrictive clauses and phrases. *A restrictive clause or phrase is needed to help identify the word it modifies (and no commas will be used).*

EXAMPLES: The girl *who is wearing a bird on her hat* does not appeal to me. (Restrictive adjective clause)

> The girl *wearing the bright green bikini* does appeal to me. (Restrictive adjective phrase)

COMMENT ON NONRESTRICTIVE CLAUSES AND PHRASES:
> *A nonrestrictive clause or phrase does **not** add anything essential to the meaning of the sentence (and commas will be used).* It may be dropped out of the sentence and not change the writer's intention.

EXAMPLES: Jim Evers, *who was coach of the football team,* had a severe headache. (Nonrestrictive adjective clause)

> Jim Evers, *wearing a bright blue suit,* walked onto the stage. (Nonrestrictive adjective phrase)

Commas

COMMENT: There are times when writers alone can decide whether they want their modifying elements to be restrictive or nonrestrictive.

EXAMPLE OF POSSIBLE RESTRICTIVE CLAUSE:

My cousin *who lives in Norwalk* is remarkably charming. (One of several cousins)

EXAMPLE OF POSSIBLE NONRESTRICTIVE CLAUSE:

My cousin, *who lives in Norwalk,* is remarkably charming. (My only cousin)

Commas

ABSOLUTE PHRASES

2 K   USE COMMAS TO SET OFF ABSOLUTE PHRASES.

EXAMPLES: *Good-natured comments on the behavior of her students having been made,* the teacher then gave them a holiday.

It was difficult for me to endure his insults, *my temper being what it is.*

COMMENT: Latin scholars will be familiar with this terminology from their knowledge of the ablative absolute. In English it is called the nominative absolute. It is a phrase grammatically independent of the independent clause but closely related to it in meaning.

(See 20F for definition of absolute phrases.)

Commas
QUOTATIONS

L USE COMMAS TO SET OFF DIRECT QUOTATIONS WITH SUCH
EXPRESSIONS AS *HE SAID, SHE ANSWERED*, ETC.

EXAMPLES: *His aunt said,* "Go to school." (Note comma is *outside*
of quotation marks.)

but

"Go to school," *his aunt said.* (Note comma is *within*
quotation marks.)

also

"It is imperative," *his aunt answered,* "that you go to
school." (Note first comma is *within* quotation marks;
the comma following *answered* is *outside* quotation
marks.)

SEE CHAPTER 5 FOR DETAILED RULES FOR QUOTATION
MARKS, THEIR PUNCTUATION, AND PARAGRAPHING.

L **2**

Commas

2 M USE COMMAS WHEN NECESSARY TO PREVENT MISREADING.

EXAMPLES: Beyond, the hills stretched majestically into the blue of the night. (The adverb *beyond* without the comma would be misread as a preposition.)

In brief, dresses will be shorter.

The boy dropped, an arrow through his heart.

Shortly after, the game warden came to arrest him.

Amanda decided to remarry, her first husband having died four years before.

After the couple had eaten, the table was cleared by the waiter.

If excessive, exercise can be harmful.

Commas

REVIEW EXERCISE   This exercise includes comma usage for rules 2A-2M.

DIRECTIONS: Copy the sentences below and insert commas where needed.

1. Pat McGee who wore a green tie complained that all his pupils were stupid silly and uncooperative.

2. "However it is obvious John" said the father to the headmaster "that parents cannot be responsible for their children's mistakes."

3. The child was accepted at Whitehall Country Day a school noted for its fine facilities pedantic teachers and pretty secretaries.

4. The goblets having been placed on the table King Arthur proposed a toast to Merlin the court astrologer.

5. Inside the house was dark dingy and dank.

6. "George for heaven's sake stop stalling" said the wife "and find out whether you were here on April 15 1935 or on June 15 1936."

7. "Yes after Hoskins completed his schooling" I remarked "he moved to 14 Barn Drive Cleveland Ohio and married Amy Stump a waitress."

8. "Taking all things into consideration Mr. Twitt" said the doctor "you are overweight overfed and I may add almost dead."

9. "After all the students have a right to speak out" remarked Mr. Flan the dean.

10. Gritting his teeth the pitcher threw the ball but he accidentally hit the batter who collapsed.

Commas

REVIEW EXERCISE   This exercise includes comma usage for the entire chapter.

DIRECTIONS: Copy the sentences below and insert commas where needed.

1.   On the day of her party Mrs. Swink bought hamburgers cole slaw ketchup chocolate cake and lemonade.

2.   Our lecture club was addressed by Wilson Tilsen M.D. who said that diet not doctors was important to good health.

3.   When spring arrives flowers begin to bloom and children are cheerful.

4.   When well behaved children can be a source of joy comfort and pride to their parents.

5.   He asked Ms. Wills his secretary "Carmen please take a letter to Willie Lohman 32 Calvin Drive Eastham Massachusetts 02642."

6.   Ellery never one to give up persisted in his studies in his sports and in his household chores.

7.   "Yes I have a question Mr. Crall" said a tall slim lady in the front row.

8.   The small hairy dog was cute it was well groomed and it was thoroughly spoiled.

9.   "I now show you this new potato peeler which you may buy for just one dollar" said the adman on TV.

10.   Having collected their tents their food and their equipment the climbers already completely exhausted began their final assault on the mountain.

Unnecessary Commas

DO NOT USE COMMAS WHEN THEY ARE NOT REQUIRED.
WHEN IN DOUBT, LEAVE THEM OUT.

COMMENT: *Circled commas in this chapter mean that they should be left out.*

A **DO NOT USE A COMMA TO SEPARATE COMPOUND NOUNS OR COMPOUND VERBS.**

COMMENT: The comma is primarily misused to separate a compound verb. Students carelessly assume that they are punctuating a compound sentence.

WRONG: Jack and Jill went up the hill ⊙ and brought back a stray cat. (*Went* and *brought* are compound verbs. There is NO punctuation here.)

WRONG: English is a language of startling beauty ⊙ and great vitality. (*Beauty* and *vitality* are compound nouns. There is NO punctuation here.)

A **3**

Unnecessary Commas

3 B DO NOT USE A COMMA BEFORE A SUBORDINATE CLAUSE WHEN IT IMMEDIATELY *FOLLOWS* THE INDEPENDENT CLAUSE.

COMMENT #1: Do not confuse this rule with *introductory* clauses and phrases. (See 2B.) The emphasis here is on a subordinate clause that *follows* an independent clause.

WRONG: She liked him ⊙ because he had muscles and was boy-boyishly egotistic.

WRONG: We will fill them up with cocktails ⊙ so that we do not have to worry about feeding them.

COMMENT #2: There may be occasions when the subordinate clause is so far away from the independent clause that a comma may be required to prevent misreading. (See 2M.)

EXAMPLE: Many parents like their children and the friends of their children, when they are watching television quietly.

Unnecessary Commas

C   **DO NOT USE A COMMA BETWEEN SUBJECT-VERB; VERB-OBJECT; ADJECTIVE-NOUN; ADVERB-ADJECTIVE-NOUN.**

COMMENT #1:   Watch out for intervening phrases between subject-verb and verb-object.

WRONG: The storm on its way across Cape Cod Bay ⊙ had an awesome beauty. (Subject *storm* and verb *had* with phrases in between)

WRONG: We saw in our horoscope ⊙ the distant future. (Verb *saw* and noun *future* as object with phrase in between)

WRONG: They all disliked the handsome, thoughtless ⊙ senator. (Adjective *thoughtless* and noun *senator*)

COMMENT #2:   In the example above, we have two adjectives in a series. (See 2E and 3D.)

WRONG: He used a flat ⊙ white enamel to decorate the baby's carriage. (Adverb *flat,* adjective *white,* and noun *enamel*)

COMMENT #3:   In the example above, *flat* is an adverb modifying *white.* It is not one of a series of adjectives. Consider: She was a *pretty* ugly girl.

c 3

Unnecessary Commas

DIRECTIONS: Copy the sentences below and remove unnecessary commas.

1. Winnie bought a shocking, pink dress for only $15.00, but the dress was too small, and did not fit.

2. The senator's wife, seized the champagne bottle, and swung it, but the bottle missed the ship, and fell into the bay.

3. Alphonse, and his date, decided to have a hamburger, because they were hungry, and had not eaten all day.

4. The girl, in the pea, green, skirt wanted to sing, while the band was playing, but her mother, would not let her.

5. Nymphs, and shepherds gaily danced, and sweetly sang in the Forest of Arden.

6. The batter clouted the ball, into the bleachers, but broke his leg, on the way to first base.

7. The small, brown, dog dashed through the front door, and jumped into the large, white, car.

8. Going to outer space, may not appeal to everyone, but the astronauts, seem to find the prospect interesting, and challenging.

9. John, took a course in anatomy, so that he could become a doctor, and make a good living.

10. The girl, in the seventh grade, decided she would become a politician, or a magician, when she grew up.

Unnecessary Commas

SERIES/CONJUNCTIONS

D DO NOT USE A COMMA BEFORE THE FIRST ITEM IN A SERIES OR AFTER THE LAST ITEM.

WRONG: He looked for⊙ beautiful, luxuriant, golden ⊙ bunches of dandelions.

WRONG: That first day of school, all the students eagerly took up the study of⊙ English, Latin, history, and algebra ⊙ in their classes.

E DO NOT USE A COMMA IN A SERIES IN WHICH *AND* OR *OR* IS USED BETWEEN THE WORDS.

WRONG: The colors consisted of pinks⊙ and golds⊙ and blues.

WRONG: Anne wanted the kitchen painted gray⊙ or pink⊙ or blue.

D
E **3**

Unnecessary Commas

RESTRICTIVES

3 F DO NOT USE COMMAS TO SET OFF RESTRICTIVE CLAUSES AND PHRASES.

WRONG: A man ⊙ *who has an appetite for living* ⊙ almost invariably likes children. (Restrictive clause)

A student ⊙ *concerned only with grades* ⊙ cannot be considered a success. (Restrictive phrase)

(See 2J for discussion of nonrestrictive clauses and phrases.)

3 G DO NOT USE COMMAS TO SET OFF RESTRICTIVE APPOSITIVES.

COMMENT: An appositional element should be considered restrictive when it so closely modifies a word that it appears to be part of the word.

WRONG: Waldo dropped in to ask his sister ⊙ Phoebe ⊙ if she had read Steinbeck's novel ⊙ *The Pearl.*

COMMENT: Almost invariably these elements follow the pattern of noun + proper noun, except where epithets such as *the Conqueror* or *the Lion-Hearted* are used.

EXAMPLES:

His son Bill		Bill, my son
My uncle Sam	but	Sam, my uncle
My Friend Flicka		Flicka, my friend
The poet Shakespeare		Shakespeare, the poet

however

Richard the Lion-Hearted
Philip the Fair
Louis the Fat

Unnecessary Commas

H **DO NOT USE A COMMA AFTER INFINITIVES, GERUNDS, OR NOUN CLAUSES USED AS SUBJECTS.**

WRONG: *To eat too many unripe apples* ⊙ can bring unpleasant consequences. (Infinitive as subject)

WRONG: *Throwing the girls into the pool* ⊙ demonstrated the manliness of the boys. (Gerund as subject)

WRONG: *That Americans eat too much and exercise too little* ⊙ is well-known in poverty-stricken countries. (Noun clause as subject)

H 3

Unnecessary Commas

3 I   **DO NOT USE A COMMA BEFORE INFINITIVES, GERUNDS, OR NOUN CLAUSES USED AS OBJECTS.**

COMMENT: This rule is an elaboration of 3C.

WRONG: I want very much⊙ *to give him the prize that he deserves.* (Infinitive as object)

WRONG: He admitted without hesitation⊙ *the stealing of his classmate's sandals.* (Gerund as object)

WRONG: Mary realized for the first time⊙ *that her mother was a human being.* (Noun clause as object)

Unnecessary Commas

3 J   DO NOT USE AN UNNECESSARY COMMA IN QUOTATIONS.

WRONG: "Come here! ⊙" the old woman shouted.

3 K   DO NOT USE A COMMA INCORRECTLY BEFORE OR AFTER PARENTHESES.

WRONG: The police arrested the boy ⊙ (he was a Harvard graduate) ⊙ last weekend.

3 L   DO NOT USE A COMMA *AFTER* COORDINATING OR CORRELATIVE CONJUNCTIONS.

WRONG: Wilma ate lunch and ⊙ then she left town.

RIGHT: Wilma ate lunch, and then she left town.

WRONG: Either he will pass or ⊙ he will punt.

RIGHT: Either he will pass, or he will punt.

Unnecessary Commas

3 DIRECTIONS: Copy the sentences below *including* all commas.
Then circle each unnecessary comma.

1. Driving a garbage truck, is not particularly inspiring work,
   but, it is steady work, and pays a good salary.

2. She knew, she would pass for the year, because she was
   on good terms with the intelligent, good-natured, headmaster.

3. The boy, who had the most money, was forced to pay for,
   the hot dogs, ice cream, and five packs of, chewing gum.

4. "Are you planning to leave now?," the father asked his small,
   impatient, son.

5. Last Easter, the bunny gave gaily, decorated eggs to all boys,
   and girls, who had been good.

6. Any student, willing to work hard, should receive
   good grades, and, make the Honor Roll.

7. He is a boy of keen intellect, and superb talent, but no coach
   wants an end, who cannot catch a football.

8. The girls gathered a variety of black, green, and yellow paper,
   so that they could redecorate the art room, and the halls.

9. He was impressed, by her grace, and her beauty, and her
   wisdom.

10. "That you are stupid, is no concern of mine!," shouted the
    irate husband.

(Continued on next page.)

Unnecessary Commas

11.   After the game, the students tore down the goal posts, and divided the pieces, among themselves.

12.   A baby, should not be disturbed, when it is crying.

13.   Brahms, (the composer), loved bucolic scenes, and often strolled in the mysterious, Black Forest.

14.   Boys, who have a strong feeling of competition, are often successful in school work, and in sports.

15.   The sound of the waves, breaking on the shore, reminds me of an old, rusty, electric shaver.

16.   That students are sometimes lazy, comes as a surprise to teachers, who always expect maximum efficiency from their pupils.

17.   It was easy to see, that Carrie did not have a chance, with the lifeguard, a dark, handsome, fellow.

18.   "I suppose, that you expect an apology?," Fiona inquired sweetly, but with hidden anger.

19.   To be successful, requires much time, and effort, and fortitude.

20.   Howard arrived at the station, as the train was leaving, but he thought, that he could catch the next one.

End Marks

4 A   USE A PERIOD AT THE END OF DECLARATIVE SENTENCES, MILD COMMANDS, AND INDIRECT STATEMENTS AND QUESTIONS.

EXAMPLES: He was a restless fellow who spent most of his time traveling. (Declarative sentence)

Go to the door, Jim, and let the salesman in. (Mild command)

I did not ask what you wanted. (Indirect question)

I know that you will always love me. (Indirect statement)

COMMENT: Always put the period *inside* quotation marks.

EXAMPLE: Mother said, "You wait until your father comes home from work."

End Marks

PERIOD/DOUBLE END MARKS

4 B   USE A PERIOD WITH MOST ABBREVIATIONS, DOLLAR SIGNS,
AND DECIMALS.

Common abbreviations:

100 A.D.	R.S.V.P.
Mr.	Mrs.
etc.	Dr.
p. 202	i.e.
P.S.	Dec.
	Ms.

The word *percent* is never followed by a period.

NOTE: ₁ Contemporary usage frequently drops periods when
they are not part of the official name. (See 9J for further
discussion of abbreviations.)

Dollar signs: $7.53 $106.73
                    but
                    53¢   73¢
Decimals: 4.8   10.3%

Do not use periods after such contractions as *I've, isn't,* etc.

4 C   NEVER USE DOUBLE END MARKS.

WRONG: He was born in 1914 A.D.⊙

WRONG: Are you sick? ⊙

WRONG: *E.T.* surely was exciting! (! !)

WRONG: Why, oh why, did I do it? (? ?)

End Marks

QUESTION MARK

4 D   USE A QUESTION MARK AT THE END OF A DIRECT QUESTION.

EXAMPLES: Why do you bother to come to school? (Direct question)

The headmaster asked, "Why do you bother to come to school?" (Direct question in quotation marks)

COMMENT #1: Put the question mark *inside* quotation marks if it is part of the quotation.

COMMENT #2: Do not use a question mark to point up a word that is supposed to be funny or ironic.

WRONG: He bowed graciously (?) and fell on his face.

COMMENT #3: Use only one question mark to denote the end of the sentence even if it is a double question.

EXAMPLE: Did Ford say, "What am I doing running for the Presidency?"

End Marks

E

USE AN EXCLAMATION POINT AFTER AN EXPRESSION OF STRONG OR SUDDEN EMOTION.

COMMENT #1: Excessive use of exclamation points, dashes, and underlining is childish. (See also 4C.)

COMMENT #2: The first word following an exclamation point begins with a capital letter.

EXAMPLE: "What a mess! Pick this room up!" he screamed.

COMMENT #3: The interjection at the beginning of an exclamatory remark will be followed either by an exclamation point or a comma. The punctuation in both examples below is correct.

EXAMPLES: Ah! There you are!

Ah, there you are!

COMMENT #4: Put the exclamation point *inside* quotation marks if it is part of the quotation.

EXAMPLE: "Well!" exclaimed the father. "So there you are!"

E 4

End Marks

4   DIRECTIONS: Copy the sentences below, supply the necessary punctuation, and remove unnecessary punctuation.

1. "Oh what a bore this class is," exclaimed Mr Philips in dismay!

2. "When will the astronaut land," asked Sgt Henry Wheeler of the U S Army?

3. "Egad what treachery" exclaimed King John as he signed the Magna Carta in 1215 A D

4. Mrs Crump asked Ms Miniver if she wanted some more chicken salad?

5. In his letter, Dr Wamma requested bandages, iodine, gauze, etc..

6. She wrote in the book report, "This was the best book I have ever read!!!"

7. At the end of her note, Mrs Calloway added, "PS. It isn't. difficult to write an RSVP".

8. "Congratulations," his boss exclaimed. "As of Sept 30, your pay will go up $300 an hour".

9. "Silence," screamed the teacher. "Why can't. you be quiet"

10. "Oh why did I ever leave Ohio," sang Miss. Russell in *Wonderful Town*

Quotation Marks

5 FOLLOW THE CONVENTIONS OF CAPITALIZATION, COMMA PLACEMENT, AND PUNCTUATION IN DIRECT QUOTATIONS.

The following examples illustrate some of the major patterns.

1. EXAMPLES OF DECLARATIVE SENTENCES:

> He said, "They arrived."
>
> "They arrived," he said.

2. EXAMPLES OF TWO INDEPENDENT DECLARATIVE SENTENCES AND INTERRUPTER VERB OF SAYING:

> "They arrived," he said. "They took baths."

3. EXAMPLE OF TWO INDEPENDENT CLAUSES, NO INTERRUPTER VERB OF SAYING:

> "They arrived. They took baths," he said.
>
> He said, "They arrived. They took baths."

4. EXAMPLE OF COMPLEX SENTENCE AND INTERRUPTER VERB OF SAYING:

> "When they arrived," he said, "they took baths."

(Continued on next page.)

5

Quotation Marks

(Examples continued)

5. EXAMPLES OF SIMPLE INTERROGATIVE SENTENCE:

He asked, "When did they arrive?"

"When did they arrive?" he asked.

6. EXAMPLE OF SIMPLE INTERROGATIVE SENTENCE AND INTERRUPTER VERB OF SAYING:

"When," he asked, "did they arrive?"

7. EXAMPLE OF TWO DIRECT QUESTIONS AND INTERRUPTER VERB OF SAYING:

"When did they arrive?" he asked. "Did they take baths?"

8. EXAMPLE OF COMPLEX INTERROGATIVE SENTENCE AND INTERRUPTER VERB OF SAYING:

"When they arrived," he asked, "did they take baths?"

9. EXAMPLE OF STRAIGHTFORWARD QUESTION AND A DIRECTLY QUOTED STATEMENT:

Did Raquel say, "I want to be loved for myself alone?"

(See 5F for question within question.)

Quotation Marks

5 A USE QUOTATION MARKS TO ENCLOSE A PERSON'S EXACT WORDS AND THOUGHTS.

      EXAMPLES: John said, "I have never enjoyed baseball."

                        Mary thought, "What am I doing here?"

      COMMENT: Do not use quotation marks with indirect statements.

      WRONG: He said, "That he was sick."

      RIGHT: He said that he was sick.

      NOTE: Quotation marks are placed next to the word to which they refer. (See also 24F.)

      WRONG: . . . . .John said,"
Come home."

      RIGHT: . . . . .John said,
"Come home."

B **BEGIN A DIRECT QUOTATION WITH A CAPITAL LETTER.**

      EXAMPLE: She wondered, "What will Daddy do now?"

5c WHEN A SENTENCE IS INTERRUPTED BY *HE SAID, SHE THOUGHT,* AND SIMILAR EXPRESSIONS, BEGIN THE SECOND PART OF THE QUOTATION WITH A SMALL LETTER.

      EXAMPLE: "The spectators scurried to the shelter," he said, "and never did return."

A
B
C
5

Quotation Marks

5 D   **IF THE SECOND PART OF THE QUOTATION BEGINS AN INDEPENDENT CLAUSE, THE FIRST WORD WILL BE CAPITALIZED. IF NOT, IT WILL BE CONSIDERED A SENTENCE ERROR.**
(See 1B.)

EXAMPLES: "I will come to the main point soon," the President said. "It will not take long."

"Come here!" Daddy cried. "Show me that report!"

(In both cases we have two independent clauses interrupted by *the President said* and *Daddy cried*. Periods must be used.)

5 E   **PLACE COMMAS AND PERIODS CLEARLY *INSIDE* QUOTATION MARKS.**

WRONG: "I will see you", he said, "when I am ready".

WRONG: "I will see you", he said, "when I am ready".

RIGHT: "I will see you," he said, "when I am ready."

Quotation Marks

DIRECTIONS: Copy the sentences below and include correct
             punctuation, correct placement of quotation marks,
             and correct capitalization.

1.   Kindly do not, said William Tell to his son. Tell your
         mother about this stolen apple.

2.   Mr. Crance asked the next-door neighbor, Where his wife
         was?"

3.   Once you have mastered your backhand ren......ed the tennis
         coach we will work on your serve.

4.   "The present did not arrive on time", said Mother,
         "it should be here tomorrow."

5.   I refuse remarked the senator to run for office. Why
         should I seek a second term.

6.   I want to see you, shouted Father, are you in the kitchen.

7.   Can you come to my party asked Miss Quince, will you bring
         the ice.

8.   The customer said that "he would rather have soup than a
         salad."

9.   "My life is a mess", Carolyn moaned. "But I think I
         have the courage to continue".

10.   Stuart suddenly heard his wife inquire, are you going to
         be home for dinner"?

Quotation Marks

5 F   **PLACE QUESTION MARKS AND EXCLAMATION POINTS INSIDE QUOTATION MARKS IF THEY ARE PART OF THE QUOTATION; OUTSIDE IF THEY ARE *NOT* PART OF THE QUOTATION.**

EXAMPLE AS PART OF THE QUOTATION:

"What are you doing?" he cried. (Question mark is within quotes)

EXAMPLE AS *NOT* PART OF QUOTATION:

Did you hear the dean say, "I won't be there"? (Question mark is outside of quotes)

BUT

Did you hear the dean say, "What am I doing here?" (One question mark will take care of both questions.)

5 G   **USE SINGLE QUOTATION MARKS TO ENCLOSE A QUOTATION WITHIN A QUOTATION.**

EXAMPLE: Ralph said, "The dean replied, 'You may not go.' " (Note the period is within quotation marks and that *The* and *You* are capitalized. Both words begin a quotation. See 5B.)

Quotation Marks

H   IN DIALOGUE BEGIN A NEW PARAGRAPH WITH EACH CHANGE OF SPEAKER.

EXAMPLE: "I don't like you," Mary said, "and I never will."
         "But you will, honey. You will," he insisted fervently and honestly.
         "Oh, go away! I never want to see you again!" the heartbroken girl cried petulantly.

I   OMIT QUOTATION MARKS AT THE END OF A PARAGRAPH WHEN THE SAME SPEAKER KEEPS ON TALKING.

EXAMPLE: "I am . . . . the Presidency . . . . today. (No quotation mark needed)
         "Moreover, I was . . . . the Indians . . . . yesterday," he said. (Quotation marks needed at the end of speech)

J   DO NOT USE QUOTATION MARKS TO ENCLOSE SLANG WORDS AND CUTE EXPRESSIONS IN FORMAL WRITING.

WRONG: The trouble with my parents is that they are "square."

WRONG: Shane is a "cool dude."
         (See also 14D.)

H
I 5
J

Quotation Marks

5 K USE QUOTATION MARKS FOR CHAPTERS OR SUBDIVISIONS OF BOOKS, TITLES OF SHORT STORIES, SONG TITLES, MAGAZINE ARTICLES, AND SHORT POEMS.

EXAMPLES: 1) "The Villain" in *Black Destiny* (chapter)
2) "In Another Country" by Ernest Hemingway (short story)
3) "Profile: Angier Biddle Duke" in *The New Yorker* (magazine article)
4) "Dulce et Decorum Est" by Wilfred Owen (short poem)
5) "You're the Cream in My Coffee" (song title)

(See 6C for use of italics.)

5 L DO NOT USE DOUBLE QUOTATION MARKS WHEN THE SAME PERSON KEEPS ON TALKING.

WRONG: "I went to the store." "I bought candy," he said.

RIGHT: "I went to the store. I bought candy," he said.

5 K
      L

Quotation Marks

5   DIRECTIONS: Copy each sentence below and include correct
punctuation, correct placement of quotation marks,
and correct capitalization.

1.   "Please be seated, ladies and gentlemen." "I have a
statement to make", said the President.

2.   Elly wondered, "Where she had left her purse?"

3.   "We will see who is right", replied Mother. "We will just
wait and see."

4.   "My car has a flat tire", said Wilma, "please come over and fix
it."

5.   "First I will finish my math", thought Willie. "And
then I will read my history."

6.   For her history assignment, Ella had to read the chapter
entitled The Composing of Our National Anthem and
memorize the words to The Star Spangled Banner.

7.   Randy heard the teacher say, "that there was no homework for
tonight."

8.   "Help me," cried the man who was going under for a third
time! I'm drowning!

9.   "Can you lend me a dime," asked Phyllis? "I have to put
some money into the parking meter".

10. Today, said the librarian. We will begin the class by trying
to find poems in the library. Who will be the first to locate
Poe's poem The Raven?

Quotation Marks

DIRECTIONS: Copy the following dialogues.
1) Insert all needed quotation marks;
2) correct all punctuation errors;
3) capitalize correctly; and
4) indent when a new paragraph is needed.

Part I

I'm so bored, said Bill, what can we do today

I don't know, replied Joe, why don't we go to a baseball game

Bill sighed and said, I'd like to go to a ball game. But I haven't any money

Joe thought a moment and said, I got my allowance yesterday, I could lend you some money

That's great, exclaimed Bill, why don't you call your parents and let them know we're going

Part II

Good morning, class, said Miss Huffle. Today we will be studying nouns." "Can anyone give me the definition of a noun?

Yes, I can, replied Ken, it's a person, place, or thing. Miss Huffle asked, is it anything else besides a person place, or thing

Yes, responded Barbie. It's an idea, too. "Very good, Barbie," said Miss Huffle.

Ken muttered, that was just a lucky guess

Part III

Bonnie sat at the table humming the last verse of When the Saints Go Marching In. "Please stop that humming, said the lady at the table next to Bonnie's.

I'm so sorry, responded Bonnie, I didn't even know I was humming. Was I disturbing you? "Yes, said the lady. Can't you see I'm trying to read this article entitled "How To Behave in Public Places"

Other Punctuation

SEMICOLON

6 A USE A SEMICOLON BETWEEN INDEPENDENT CLAUSES NOT JOINED BY COORDINATING CONJUNCTIONS.

COMMENT #1: Semicolons separate clauses more decisively than does the comma, but without the finality of a period.

COMMENT #2: Failure to follow this rule constitutes a SENTENCE ERROR. (See 1G.)

EXAMPLE: It was the final day of school; even the teachers were exhilarated.

NOTE: Semicolons should be used sparingly and with caution.

BE PARTICULARLY CAREFUL TO USE A SEMICOLON BETWEEN INDEPENDENT CLAUSES JOINED BY CONJUNCTIVE ADVERBS OR BY TRANSITIONAL PHRASES.

Conjunctive adverbs:
also, anyhow, besides, furthermore, however, indeed, instead, meanwhile, moreover, nevertheless, otherwise, still, then, therefore

EXAMPLE WITH CONJUNCTIVE ADVERB:
We took a bus to New York City; *then* we transferred to the subway to reach Lincoln Center.

Transitional phrases:
in fact, on the contrary, on the other hand, that is, first, second, as a result, for instance, consequently, at this time

EXAMPLE WITH TRANSITIONAL PHRASE:
An Irish breakfast is delicious; *in fact,* it puts the continental breakfast to shame.

Other Punctuation

6 B **USE A SEMICOLON TO SEPARATE ITEMS IN A SERIES THAT ALREADY CONTAIN COMMAS.**

EXAMPLES: The meeting was attended by Jonas, the mayor; Willis, the treasurer; and Henley, the social secretary.

The barn was erected by Mr. Levis, who supplied the wood ; Mr. Crunde, who donated the nails; and Mr. Ellis, who was an expert carpenter.

Other Punctuation

EXERCISE

DIRECTIONS: Copy the sentences below and insert semicolons where
needed.

1.   He owns vast tracts of land in Canada moreover, his wife owns
a ranch in Texas.

2.   Gorman loved candy in fact, he ate so much of it that he became sick.

3.   Amy left the airport at noon then she drove home.

4.   Karl decided not to buy the fiddle instead he bought an electric guitar.

5.   Ice cream is delicious on the other hand, it is fattening.

6.   Queen Elizabeth II is wealthy moreover, she is popular.

7.   You must learn not to be messy first wipe the grape juice off
the rug.

8.   The three musicians were Karl, a fiddler, Al, a drummer, and
Emmy, a singer.

9.   Three boats broke the club record: *Bluefish,* first place,
Dolphin, second place, and *Guppie,* third place.

10.   A detective, Sherlock Holmes, his friend, Doctor Watson,
and Professor Moriarty, the villain, were the main
characters in the book.

Other Punctuation

6 c   UNDERLINE (ITALICIZE):

         1) TITLES OF BOOKS, MAGAZINES, MOTION
PICTURES, PLAYS, TV PROGRAMS, NEWSPAPERS

         2) WORKS OF ART, MUSIC.

         3) NAMES OF SHIPS, TRAINS, AIRPLANES,
SPACECRAFT.

         4) WORDS OF FOREIGN LANGUAGES.

         5) WORDS, LETTERS, OR NUMBERS REFERRED
TO BY NAME.

COMMENT #1:   Handwritten and typed copy must be underlined to
designate italics for the printer.

EXAMPLE OF HANDWRITTEN AND TYPED COPY:

We like The Saturday Evening Post.

EXAMPLE OF PRINTER'S ITALICS:

We like *The Saturday Evening Post.*

COMMENT #2:   Use quotation marks only for chapters or subdivisions
of books, titles of short stories, song titles, magazine
articles, and short poems. (See 5K.)

COMMENT #3:   The Bible (and its parts) is *never* underlined nor en-
enclosed in quotation marks.

EXAMPLES OF TITLES:

Tom Sawyer (novel), *Gone with the Wind* (movie), *Har-
per's Magazine* (magazine), *The New York Times* (newspaper), *Funk and Wagnalls Standard College Dictionary*
(reference), *Harbrace College Handbook* (textbook), *As
the World Turns* (TV program).

Other Punctuation

ITALICS

EXAMPLES OF SHIPS, TRAINS, AIRPLANES, SPACECRAFT:

The *Queen Mary* (ship), *Old Ironsides* (ship), the *Merchants Limited* (train), the *Spirit of St. Louis* (airplane), *Columbia* and *Challenger* (spacecraft)

EXAMPLES OF WORKS OF MUSIC, ART:

> Beethoven's *Pastoral Symphony* (music), Leonardo's *Last Supper* (art)

EXAMPLES OF FOREIGN WORDS:

> *Faux pas, cherchez la femme, nyet, élan*

EXAMPLES OF WORDS, LETTERS, NUMERALS REFERRED TO BY NAME:

> The word *get* has lost most of its force.

> The letter *e* is not pronounced in *alone.*

> Many of us consider *13* an unlucky number.

C 6

Other Punctuation

COLON

6 D   USE A COLON (1) TO INTRODUCE A LIST OR SERIES OR (2) TO INTRODUCE A LONG FORMAL QUOTATION.

COMMENT: Basically the colon takes the place of such expressions as *thus, namely, for example, such as, as follows.*

EXAMPLES: There are three kinds of students: the lazy, the indifferent, and the industrious. (A series)

The Quaker, William Penn, wrote: "To be innocent is to not be guilty; but to be virtuous is to overcome our evil inclinations." (A long formal quotation)

NOTE: If a complete sentence follows the colon, capitalize the first word. If a word, a series of words, or phrases follow the colon, do *not* capitalize the first word.

Other Punctuation

COLON

E **USE THE COLON FOLLOWING THE SALUTATION OF A LETTER, TO SEPARATE HOURS FROM MINUTES, AND TO SEPARATE CHAPTER AND VERSE IN THE BIBLE.**

EXAMPLES: Dear Mr. Smith:

3:17 P.M. (or 3:17 p.m.)

The Sermon on the Mount begins with Matthew 5:1.

6 F **DO NOT USE A COLON IN PLACE OF A COMMA.**

COMMENT: Colons may be used to introduce formal quotations (see 6D) but *not* in dialogue.

WRONG: John said: "Here I come, ready or not."

RIGHT: John said, "Here I come, ready or not."

69

E
F 6

Other Punctuation

6 G   **USE THE DASH ONLY TO INDICATE A VERY SUDDEN BREAK OR CHANGE IN THOUGHT.**

COMMENT: The dash is primarily used to bring emphatically to the reader's attention parenthetical material that generally is set off by commas, parentheses, or brackets. However, it should be avoided in formal writing. Even in informal writing, its overuse is childish.

EXAMPLES:

To separate a parenthetical expression from main clause:

As a matter of fact, she was always true to him — in her fashion.

Mrs. Atwood took thirty minutes to explain — she had a serious case of logorrhea — the gruesome details of her latest operation.

To set off a word or words in lengthy apposition:

I saw that man from Boston yesterday — Mr. Jones, I think his name was.

The three of them — George, John, and Bill — all went to college at the same time.

Other Punctuation

PARENTHESES

H USE PARENTHESES (1) TO ENCLOSE EXPLANATORY AND ILLUSTRATIVE MATERIAL THAT IS ADDED TO A SENTENCE OR (2) TO ENCLOSE NUMERALS (AS IN THIS RULE).

COMMENT #1: Punctuation belonging to the main part of the sentence is placed outside the closing parenthesis.

EXAMPLE: He had a long life (1870-1968); he was loved by friend and foe.

COMMENT #2: Parenthetical elements do not strictly belong within the grammatical structure of the sentence, which ought to read clearly without such marks.

EXAMPLES: Agatha made it clear to her psychiatrist that she liked sweets (chewing gum), dolls (the more bedraggled the better), and the opposite sex (particularly boys).

Henry David Thoreau (1817-62) was one of our great American writers.

He outlined three things we had to do: (1) collect the money, (2) give a sample of our product, and (3) depart from town as quickly as possible.

I DO NOT USE PARENTHESES INSTEAD OF COMMAS.

WRONG: I visited Bill (my brother) in jail.

CORRECTED
SENTENCE: I visited Bill, my brother, in jail.

H
I 6

Other Punctuation

BRACKETS

6 J USE BRACKETS (1) TO SET OFF ERRORS OR (2) EDITORIAL ADDITIONS IN THE TEXT AND (3) TO ENCLOSE PARENTHESES WITHIN PARENTHESES.

EXAMPLE TO SHOW ERROR IN TEXT:

>   She was much to [sic] fat.

NOTE: The *sic* (meaning *thus* from the Latin) is a favorite device of editors to show that the error is not theirs but that of the original writer — and so not a misprint.

EXAMPLE TO SHOW ADDITION TO TEXT:

>   He wrote Walter [Walter Smith] a note, but he never replied.

EXAMPLE OF PARENTHESES WITHIN PARENTHESES:

WRONG: She enjoyed classical music (particularly the symphonies of Beethoven (1770-1827)).

CORRECTED SENTENCE: She enjoyed classical music (particularly the symphonies of Beethoven [1770-1827]).

Other Punctuation

DIRECTIONS: Copy the sentences below and insert the necessary punctuation (i.e., semicolon, italics, colon, dash, parentheses, brackets). You may remove commas where other punctuation is required.

1. Dr. Faustus, a play by Christopher Marlowe, is a fine play, Julius Caesar, by William Shakespeare, is even better.

2. He usually drove to his office in New York, however, he decided for a change to take the 8 22 milk train from Greenwich.

3. Dear Mr. Cogway
    Thank you for your inquiry regarding my article titled The Bible Today which appeared in The New Yorker magazine.
    I think you will find that I have quoted correctly from the Bible, Genesis 1 1, In the beginning God created the heaven and the earth.

4. English teachers abhor the word fun used as an adjective, furthermore, they abhor students who use this word.

5. John F. Kennedy, 1917-63, often used the yacht Honey Fitz to entertain visiting statesmen.

6. If you continue to pull out your hair, I don't know why you began the habit, you will be bald in six months.

(Continued on next page.)

Other Punctuation

(Continued)

6

7. The passengers with pea-green faces aboard the Queen of the Sea suffered from a sickness that the French call mal de mer.

8. Michelangelo's Pieta a statue known throughout the world is on view at the Vatican in Rome.

9. She recognized three kinds of animals, fish, swimming creatures, birds, flying creatures, and mammals, walking creatures.

10. The first movement of Haydn's Surprise Symphony is divided into three parts, 1 a slow introduction, 2 a thematic section, and 3 a development section.

11. James Thurber wrote in the book Further Fables for Our Time, All men should strive to learn before they die what they are running from, and to, and why.

12. Mae's uncle (who had played a small part in General Hospital) wrote her: "I am mush (sic) happier now."

13. Mr. Omelette, do you spell your last name with an E or an O?

14. He read in The Washington Post,"The gerilla sic is the largest, and perhaps the smelliest, member of the ape family."

15. Cora was a genius, indeed, she received 100 on every exam she ever took.

Capitals

7 A CAPITALIZE THE FIRST WORD OF EVERY SENTENCE.

7 B CAPITALIZE THE FIRST WORD OF A DIRECT QUOTATION UNLESS IT IS THE FIRST WORD OF A QUOTED SENTENCE FRAGMENT.

EXAMPLE: Mary said, "Come home, Johnny."

but

"Come home, Johnny," Mary said, "and wash the dishes."

C CAPITALIZE THE FIRST WORD OF A FORMAL STATEMENT FOLLOWING A COLON.

EXAMPLE: The press release of President Kennedy proclaimed: "We the people of this nation are a united people." (See also 6F.)

D CAPITALIZE THE FIRST WORD IN EVERY LINE OF POETRY (UNLESS POET'S PERSONAL PREFERENCE DIRECTS OTHERWISE).
EXAMPLE: Not any sunny tone
From any fervent zone
Finds entrance there.

E CAPITALIZE THE FIRST WORD OF EACH TOPIC IN AN OUTLINE. (See Appendix 8, p.263.)

A
B
C
D
E

7

Capitals

CAPITALIZE:
      1) **PROPER NOUNS AND PROPER ADJECTIVES.**
      2) **TITLES OF DISTINCTION.**
      3) **IMPORTANT WORDS IN TITLES OF PUBLICATIONS**
      4) **REFERENCES TO DEITY.**

Proper names: Shakespeare, Texas, America

Proper adjectives: Shakespearean, Texan, American

Races, cultural groups, religions: **C**aucasian, **P**rotestant, **J**ew, **C**atholicism, **I**ndian

Wars and battles: World War I, the Battle of Bull Run

Geographic divisions: the **E**ast **R**iver, Mount Ararat, the **M**idwest, **F**ifth **A**venue, North Street

Days and months: Saturday, July

Companies, organizations, clubs, buildings: the **F**ord **M**otor **C**ompany, the **Y**oung **M**en's **C**hristian Association, the **R**otary **C**lub, the **E**mpire **S**tate **B**uilding

Official bodies: the **C**ongress, the **T**reasury **D**epartment

Deity: God, Buddha, Zeus, Eros

NOTE: Capitalize pronouns and adjectives that refer to the Deity.

       God in **H**is (adjective) wisdom knows what **H**e (pronoun) is doing.

Capitals

(Continued)

Titles of publications: *The New York Times, The Last of the Mohicans, A Day on the River*

Titles of distinction: the **B**ishop of Connecticut, the **D**uke of Greenwich, the **Q**ueen of England, the **P**resident of the United States (See 7H-7J for words not capitalized.)

Specific courses: English, Spanish, Algebra I, Economics 10

Trade names: Coke, Jeep, Frigidaire, Band-Aid

COMMENT: When in doubt about capitalization, consult a dictionary.

Capitals

7 G CAPITALIZE THE PRONOUN *I* AND THE INTERJECTION *O*.

EXAMPLE: "Where, **O** where has my little dog gone?" **I** asked.

7 H **DO NOT CAPITALIZE GENERAL OR CLASS NAMES, GEOGRAPHICAL DIRECTIONS, THE SEASONS.**

COMMENT: The italicized words below are not to be capitalized.

EXAMPLES: Martin Luther King was an important *black* leader.

Paula was elected *president* of her class.

My dog is a *spaniel.*

We drove *east* to Main Street.

I was born in the *summer.*

I studied *mathematics, history,* and *algebra.*

He is a *freshman* at Yale.

7 I **DO NOT USE CAPITALS REFERRING TO FAMILY RELATIONSHIPS WHEN THEY ARE PRECEDED BY A POSSESSIVE.**

EXAMPLES: My *mother* is always late.

but

When is *Mother* coming?

7 **G**
H
I

Capitals

J   **DO NOT CAPITALIZE ARTICLES AND PREPOSITIONS IN TITLES, UNLESS THEY ARE THE FIRST WORDS OF THE TITLE.**

EXAMPLES: My Ride on the Subway (*on, the* not capitalized)

The Man on the Flying Trapeze (*The* capitalized, *on* and *the* not capitalized)

NOTE: Prepositions and conjunctions of five letters or over in titles are, by editorial convention, capitalized.

Hence:

The Man Without a Country (*Without* capitalized, but *a* not capitalized)

7 K   **DO NOT CARELESSLY CAPITALIZE WORDS THAT NEED NO CAPITALS.**

WRONG: We took our *Packs* off *Because* we were tired.

RIGHT: We took our *packs* off *because* we were tired.

J
K 7

Capitals

7   DIRECTIONS: Copy the sentences below. Capitalize words requiring capitals, and correct words that are improperly capitalized.

1. On friday, june 6, my Father and Mother bought me a Boston Bull Terrier.

2. *the bridge on the river kwai* was shown to the prince of wales last Winter.

3. "Joe, bring me a copy of webster's dictionary," said father. "This Puzzle is difficult."

4. After the battle of gettysburg in southern pennsylvania, president lincoln delivered his famous address that began, "four score and seven years ago . . ."

5. the lawyer from new england was elected to the united states senate for four consecutive terms.

6. "You go East past the havermeyer building," said my Brother, "And then turn South on Greenwich Avenue until you reach manero's restaurant."

7. The president of the fairfield garden club won first prize with her dorothy perkins roses.

8. Jesus took his followers, and he went into jerusalem.

9. The senate was told by president reagan that indians, being equal to whites in eyes of god, should have equal rights in america.

Capitals

10. The american troops met bitter resistance from the germans in the battle of the bulge during world war II.

11. When jerry was a senior, he studied Biology, Mathematics, english, and french.

12. During the reign of queen elizabeth I, shakespeare and his Fellow playwrights wrote dramas that showed great National Pride.

13. The great australian explorer, sir alfred quimby, was responsible for discovering the Nutritional Value of spanish seaweed.

14. Mercutio said to romeo, "o, then i see that queen mab hath been with you."

15. Said atilla the hun to the pope, "I am neither catholic, protestant, nor jew."

16. Dorothy parker wrote: "men seldom make passes at girls who wear glasses."

17. "I enjoyed the book *gone with the wind*," Martha said, "but i liked *men without women* even more."

18. Outline: I. after the thunder storm
              A. rain on the streets
              B. water in the gutters
              C. birds on the wing

Apostrophes

8 A USE THE APPROPRIATE FORM OF THE APOSTROPHE TO FORM THE POSSESSIVE CASE OF A NOUN OR AN INDEFINITE PRONOUN.

Possessive singular

    The girl's hats

    The man's hats

    *Jones's cat (or Jones' cat)

    *Merriss's car (or Merriss' car)

    *(See possible exceptions, 8B.)

Possessive plural

    The girls' hats

    The men's hats

    The Joneses' cat

    The Merrisses' car

Group possessive

    John and Mary's house (joint ownership)

    men and women's goal (joint ownership)

    Bill's and Mary's parents (individual ownership)

    everybody's and Jim's cat (individual ownership)

8 B **TO FORM THE POSSESSIVE SINGULAR, ADD 'S.**
(See Strunk and White for authority.)

(See 8A above.)

POSSIBLE EXCEPTIONS: Names already ending with an *s*-sound where adding an apostrophe with the *s* would make the pronunciation awkward: Dickens' novels, Ulysses' voyage, Socrates' philosophy.

8 C **TO FORM THE POSSESSIVE PLURAL, ADD ONLY THE APOSTROPHE WHEN IT ENDS IN *S*. IF IT DOES NOT END IN *S*, ADD 'S.**

(See 8A above.)

8
A
B
C

Apostrophes

D TO FORM THE POSSESSIVE PLURAL IN JOINT OWNERSHIP, ADD *'S* TO THE LAST WORD.

(See 8A, p. 82.)

8 E TO SHOW INDIVIDUAL OWNERSHIP WITH COMPOUNDED WORDS, ADD *'S* TO EACH WORD.

(See 8A, p. 82.)

8 F USE THE APOSTROPHE TO SHOW THE POSSESSIVE CASE WHEN NOUNS ARE USED WITH GERUNDS.

EXAMPLES: Mary's swimming of the Atlantic . . .

The men's shooting of the dog . . .

D
E
F **8**

Apostrophes

8 G   USE THE APOSTROPHE IN CERTAIN IDIOMATIC EXPRESSIONS.

EXAMPLES: Today's lesson
Childhood's end
A stone's throw
Eight cents' worth

8 H   USE THE APOSTROPHE TO INDICATE THE OMISSION OF LETTERS OR FIGURES.

EXAMPLES: it's (for *it is* only), can't, he's, you're, 'tis, o'clock (of the clock), class of '65.

NOTE: Make sure to place the apostrophe where the omission occurs.

WRONG: is'nt   have'nt

RIGHT: isn't   haven't

8 I   USE THE APOSTROPHE TO FORM THE PLURAL OF NUMBERS, LETTERS, AND WORDS REFERRED TO BY NAME.

EXAMPLES: Dot your *i*'s and cross your *t*'s.

Make sure your *9*'s do not look like *7*'s.

She used too many *and*'s and *but*'s in her composition.

Apostrophes

8 J   DO NOT USE AN APOSTROPHE WITH POSSESSIVE ADJECTIVES OR PRONOUNS.

       EXAMPLES: its (when not *it is*), hers, ours, theirs, yours

       COMMENT: Usage now steers away from using the apostrophe and the possessive case with inanimate objects. Use a prepositional phrase.

       EXAMPLES: The roofs of the house (*not* the house's roofs)

                       The gypsy moths of the forest (*not* the forest's gypsy moths)

8 K   DO NOT USE 'S FOR THE PLURAL OR FOR VERBS.

       WRONG: He wished the *parent's* of the boys *lot's* of luck.

       RIGHT: He wished the *parents* of the boys *lots* of luck.

       WRONG: The baby just *run's* and *play's* all day.

       RIGHT: The baby just *runs* and *plays* all day.

8 L   AVOID THE USE OF THE APOSTROPHE AS A CONTRACTION IN FORMAL WRITING.

       AVOID: The philosophers Whitehead and Russell *aren't* studied today.

       BETTER: The philosophers Whitehead and Russell *are not* studied today.

Apostrophes

DIRECTIONS: Copy the sentences below and insert necessary apostrophes and *s*'s and omit unnecessary apostrophes.

1. Theres no reason to visit the Oshkosh Mens Club tonight at eight oclock.

2. Mr. and Mrs. Davis pet ocelot has lost it's collar, and the police cant find it.

3. Hamlets speech, "Tis now the very witching time of night," appealed to the audiences emotions.

4. "Mind you're ps and qs," said the teacher, "and the world is your's."

5. "Your uncle just sit's around all day and read's newspapers and magazine's," complained Aunt Sylvia, my mothers sister.

6. Rudolphs rendition of "Your's is My Heart Alone" cleared the room of listener's.

7. Megs winning of the scholarship prize took a years work and month's of concentration.

8. Its essential that scholar's of the Civil War read Stowes novel *Uncle Toms Cabin.*

9. The college president began the formal presentation by saying, "Let's remember all the member's of the class of 51 who've passed away."

(Continued on next page.)

Apostrophes

10. The Workmens Club was angered by Senator Moss' stand on workers salaries.

11. One of the advertisement's in the yearbook read, "Lot's of luck to the class of 66."

12. In Las Vegas Thunderbird Hotel, I heard a woman at the poker table say, "I have three 9s and two 6s."

13. "Wheres Princetons coach?" he asked.

14. I answered, "He's at the Frenches house having shepherds pie."

15. James voice could be heard above the peoples chatter, "Lord and Taylors third floor! Ladies hosiery! Childrens toys! Its bargain day!"

16. Todays sermon will be titled, "Our's, Your's, and Mine."

17. Mrs. Phillips dog ate some of the neighbors roses.

18. The events of the 1850s led to Lincolns election in 1860.

19. "What will the nurse's think?" asked Doctor Jones' secretary.

20. Joshua could'nt remember whether he was in the class of 60 or 61.

Miscellaneous Mechanics

HYPHENS

9 A   **USE A HYPHEN TO JOIN TWO OR MORE WORDS TO FORM SINGLE ADJECTIVES BEFORE A NOUN.**

EXAMPLES: *hard-fisted* tyrant
devil-may-care approach to life

COMMENT: Keep in mind that the chief function of the hyphen is to show that two or more words are to be read together as a single word, which then ends up with its own meaning.

COMPARE: He was a *child killer.* (As a child, he killed.)

He was a *child-killer.* (He killed children.)

9 B   **AVOID OVERUSE OF THE HYPHEN.**

COMMENT #1:   The best way to determine whether or not a word is hyphenated is to use your dictionary, remembering that no two dictionaries agree. The rules in this section, however, can be useful.

COMMENT #2:   When the adjective follows the noun, the hyphen is usually omitted.

EXAMPLES: *after-school* tea *but* tea after school
dark-colored glasses *but* glasses of a dark color
a *first-rate* student *but* a student who is first rate

COMMENT #3:   Some adjectives joined to participles are hyphenated both when they precede and follow a noun.

EXAMPLES: A *worm-eaten* turnip *will also be* a turnip that is *worm-eaten.*

A *hard-working* student *may also be* a student who is *hard-working.*

Miscellaneous Mechanics

C USE A HYPHEN WITH A COMPOUND NUMBER FROM TWENTY-ONE TO NINETY-NINE AND WITH FRACTIONS USED AS ADJECTIVES BEFORE THE WORD THEY MODIFY.

EXAMPLES: *twenty-three* pirates, *thirty-nine* steps
a *two-thirds* majority *but* a majority of two thirds
one-third full *but* He ate one third of the rice.

D USE A HYPHEN WITH THE PREFIXES *EX-, SELF-, ALL-,* AND WITH THE SUFFIX *-ELECT* JOINED TO NOUNS.

EXAMPLES: *ex-president*   *all-purpose*
self-made   *governor-elect*

E USE A HYPHEN WHEN DIVIDING A WORD INTO SYLLABLES, PARTICULARLY WHEN IT DOES NOT FIT AT THE END OF A LINE OF WRITING OR TYPESCRIPT. NEVER DIVIDE A ONE-SYLLABLE WORD. WHEN IN DOUBT, USE A DICTIONARY.

COMMENT: Hyphens go at the end of the line — not at the beginning of the next line. (See 24B, 24C, 24D, and 24I.)

C
D
E
9

Miscellaneous Mechanics

HYPHENS

9 F   SOME ADJECTIVES AND NOUNS ARE HYPHENATED FOLLOWING NO RULES. USE A DICTIONARY.

EXAMPLES: *flat-footed, old-fashioned, long-legged, good-natured, father-in-law, great-uncle* but *godfather, half brother, stepmother*

EXERCISE ON HYPHENS:

Using a dictionary, spell the following words correctly:

knee high	dog in the manger
land poor	dog legged
science fiction	dog paddle
parapsychology	dog's age
hard headed	horse and buggy
pro Communist	horselaugh
pepper mill	do it yourself kit
non stop	do or die attempt
up to date	bedroom suburb
all German talks	great grandfather
happy go lucky	light hearted

Miscellaneous Mechanics

ABBREVIATIONS

9 G ALWAYS USE THE CORRECT ABBREVIATIONS.

EXAMPLES: TV (not T.V.)   World War II (not WW II)
U.S.A. (not Usa)

9 H ABBREVIATE TITLES BEFORE NAMES.

EXAMPLES: *Mr.* Thomas Smith; *Dr.* Jones; The *Hon.* John Bates;
Ms. Wendy Brooks.

NOTE: The word *Miss* (as in *Miss Jones*) is not an abbreviation.

but

If the title is followed by the *last name* only, it must be written out.

EXAMPLE: Prof. Max Pryor becomes *Professor* Pryor
Gen. Mark Cross becomes *General* Cross

9 I ABBREVIATE DESIGNATIONS AFTER NAMES.

EXAMPLES: John Jones, *M.D.*; Thomas Smith, *Jr.*; The Rev. Harry
Brown, *L.L.D.*

9 J YOU MAY ABBREVIATE MONTHS, STATES, ORGANIZATIONS,
AND OTHER CONVENTIONALLY ACCEPTED TERMS.

NOTE: Some abbreviations no longer use periods. When in doubt,
use a dictionary.

Some abbreviations with periods:		Some abbreviations without periods:
C.O.D.		WQXR
a.m.		CBS
p.m.		NBC
A.D.		NFL
B.C.		TWA
Co.		TV
Sept.		UN
*Mass.	or	*MA
*Conn.	or	*CT
*Cal.	or	*CA

(Postal Service abbreviations)

*NOTE: States may be abbreviated with or without periods.

G
H
I
J
9

Miscellaneous Mechanics

NUMBERS

9 K   **WRITE OUT NUMBERS OF ONE OR TWO WORDS. USE NUMERALS FOR OTHER NUMBERS.**

    EXAMPLES: *seven* dollars, *forty-five* cents, *four million* people
                 but 1965; 1,233,650; $34.15

9 L   **WRITE OUT ORDINAL NUMBERS (ENDING IN *ST, ND, RD, TH*) UNLESS STREET NUMBERS.**

    EXAMPLES: I was *second* (not *2nd*) in line on the *third* (not *3rd*) escalator.

                 July fourth *or* July 4 (not *July 4th*)

                 Thirty-fourth Street *or* 34th Street

9 M   **DO NOT BEGIN A SENTENCE WITH NUMERALS. IF NECESSARY, REWRITE THE SENTENCE.**

    WRONG: 8 boys came.

    RIGHT: *Eight* boys came.

    WRONG: 3,562,100 votes were cast.

    RIGHT: The citizens cast 3,562,100 votes.

Miscellaneous Mechanics

NUMBERS

9 N   USE NUMERALS:

For dates: April 1, 1965; 10 B.C.; 617 A.D.

For time: 6:00 a.m. *also* six o'clock

After No. (number): Box No. 26

After p. and pp. (page, pages): p. 19; pp. 23-26

After dollar signs: $12.63

With street numbers and zip code: 26 Fairfield Road; 06830

With telephone numbers: 661-9878

With percentages and decimals: 10%; .012

CARET

9 O   USE THE CARET PROPERLY TO INSERT A WORD THAT HAS BEEN OMITTED.

NOTE: Use the caret correctly. Avoid its overuse.

WRONG: My father ⌄ is sick.   WRONG: My father ^ is sick.

RIGHT: My father is ^ sick.

9 P   DO NOT USE *ETC.*, **&**, AND *PLUS*.
(See also 14J.)

Miscellaneous Mechanics

REVIEW
EXERCISE

9 DIRECTIONS: Copy the sentences below and correct all errors
in mechanics.

1. On July 4th, the exgovernor of Ohio made a half
-hearted effort to deliver a speech.

2. 15 members of our class told Miss. Warner that they had
watched T.V. last night & had not completed their homework.

3. They wrote a letter to Prof. Smillens stating their
objections in a good natured way.

4. Ms Cole had a 2nd helping of quiche plus a rich dessert,
coffee, mints, etc.

5. 3 hours later, at exactly 5 o'clock pm, an agent from the
N.F.L. showed up at Seven Willow Street.

6. Walker arrived with his 3rd wife, a self made woman who
headed one of the largest companies in the USA.

7. The hardworking house maid used an all purpose cleaner
to wash up after working 8 hours.

8. The chief said there were 4,000 members of his tribe,
all of whom were firstrate hunters.

9. In nineteen hundred AD, Terrence Cox, Jr, was born, & 6
years later his father died.

10. The President elect announced a new program to deal with
the 1000's of Americans who were on welfare.

Case

USE THE CORRECT CASE OF NOUNS AND PRONOUNS.

There are three cases in English: the nominative, the objective, and the possessive.

Uses of the Nominative

1. Subject of a verb
2. Predicate nominative
3. Word in direct address
4. Apposition to another word in nominative case

Uses of the Objective

1. Direct object of a verb
2. Indirect object of a verb
3. Object of a preposition
4. Subject of an infinitive
5. Apposition to another word in objective case

Uses of the Possessive

1. Ownership (Mary's hat)
2. Close connection (a day's march, ten cents' worth)

(Continued on next page.)

10

Case

10

COMMENT: Most of the trouble with cases stems from the misuse of personal pronouns and of certain relative and interrogative pronouns. Learn them.

Personal Pronouns

Singular

	First person	*Second person*	*Third person*
Nom.	I	you	he, she, it
Poss.	my, mine	your, yours	his, hers, its
Obj.	me	you	him, her, it

Plural

Nom.	we	you	they
Poss.	our, ours	your, yours	their, theirs
Obj.	us	you	them

Relative and Interrogative Pronouns

Singular and Plural

Nom.	who	whoever	which	that
Poss.	whose	whosever	which	that
Obj.	whom	whomever	which	that

10

Case

NOMINATIVE

A PRONOUNS USE THE NOMINATIVE CASE WHEN USED AS SUBJECTS.

B PRONOUNS USE THE NOMINATIVE CASE WHEN USED AS SUBJECTS IN COMPOUND CONSTRUCTIONS.

WRONG: *Me* and my brother toured Park Avenue.

RIGHT: My brother and *I* toured Park Avenue.

NOTE: The first person pronoun must come *last,* not first, in compound constructions.

C PRONOUNS USE THE NOMINATIVE CASE WHEN USED AS SUBJECTS IN APPOSITIONAL CONSTRUCTIONS.

WRONG: *Us* schoolgirls enjoy chewing gum on the sly.

RIGHT: *We* schoolgirls enjoy chewing gum on the sly.

COMMENT: In the sentence above, *schoolgirls* is an appositive to *we.*

D PRONOUNS USE THE NOMINATIVE CASE WHEN USED IN THE PREDICATE NOMINATIVE OR WITH EXPLETIVES.

COMMENT: The verb *to be* is always followed by the nominative case. It is called the *predicate nominative.*

WRONG: Did you think Frank was *him*?

RIGHT: Did you think Frank was *he*?

(Continued on next page.)

97

A
B
C
D
10

Case

         NOMINATIVE

WRONG: Did you think it was *him*?

RIGHT: Did you think it was *he*?

NOTE: In the sentence above, *it* is an expletive; *he* is the subject of the clause.

10 E   RELATIVE AND INTERROGATIVE PRONOUNS USE THE NOMINATIVE CASE WHEN USED AS SUBJECTS IN THEIR OWN CLAUSES.

WRONG: *Whom* do you think you are?

RIGHT: *Who* do you think you are?

NOTE: In the sentence above, *who* is the predicate noun and refers to subject *you*.

WRONG: I know *whom* it must have been.

RIGHT: I know *who* it must have been.

NOTE: In the sentence above, *it* is an expletive. *Who* is subject of verb *must have been*.

10 F   PRONOUNS USE THE NOMINATIVE CASE WHEN USED AS SUBJECTS IN ELLIPTICAL* CONSTRUCTIONS.

WRONG: He is lazier than *me*.

RIGHT: He is lazier than *I*.

*NOTE: *Ellipsis* is an omission of a word or several words. The context, however, remains clear.

EXAMPLE: He is lazier than I [*am*].

Case

G PRONOUNS USE THE OBJECTIVE CASE WHEN USED AS DIRECT OBJECTS.

H PRONOUNS USE THE OBJECTIVE CASE WHEN USED AS DIRECT OBJECTS IN COMPOUND CONSTRUCTIONS.

WRONG: The ball hit Dick and *I.*

RIGHT: The ball hit Dick and *me.*   (Not *me and Dick*: personal pronouns come *last.*)

I PRONOUNS USE THE OBJECTIVE CASE WHEN USED AS INDIRECT OBJECTS.

WRONG: Tony gave *she* a beautiful gift.

RIGHT: Tony gave *her* a beautiful gift.

J PRONOUNS USE THE OBJECTIVE CASE WHEN USED AS INDIRECT OBJECTS IN COMPOUND CONSTRUCTIONS.

WRONG: Rex gave Jo and *I* some candy.

RIGHT: Rex gave Jo and *me* some candy.
(Not *me and Jo*: personal pronouns come *last.*)

NOTE: When two or more pronouns are used as indirect objects in compound constructions, the pronouns will use the objective case.

WRONG: Ira gave *she* and *I* some glue.

RIGHT: Ira gave *her* and *me* some glue.

G
H
I
J
10

Case

10 K **PRONOUNS USE THE OBJECTIVE CASE WHEN USED AS OBJECTS OF PREPOSITIONS.**

WRONG: Between you and *I*, this food is inedible.

RIGHT: Between you and *me*, this food is inedible.

(Not *me and you*: personal pronouns come *last*.)

10 L **PRONOUNS USE THE OBJECTIVE CASE WHEN IN APPOSITIONAL CONSTRUCTIONS.**

WRONG: The coach liked only two boys, Tom and *I*.

RIGHT: The coach liked only two boys, Tom and *me*.

(Not *me and Tom*: personal pronouns come *last*.)

10 M **PRONOUNS USE THE OBJECTIVE CASE WHEN USED AS DIRECT OBJECTS IN ELLIPTICAL CONSTRUCTIONS.**
(See 10F.)

WRONG: She kissed Tom more fervently than [she kissed] *I*.

RIGHT: She kissed Tom more fervently than [she kissed] *me*.

10 N **PRONOUNS USE THE OBJECTIVE CASE AS SUBJECTS OF THE INFINITIVE.**

RIGHT: I want *her* to do my errands.

RIGHT: They wanted *him* to be the one chosen.

10 O **RELATIVE AND INTERROGATIVE PRONOUNS USE THE OBJECTIVE CASE WHEN USED AS OBJECTS IN THEIR OWN CLAUSES.**

WRONG: *Who* did you see?

RIGHT: *Whom* did you see?

WRONG: *Who* did you look for?

RIGHT: *Whom* did you look for?

10
K
L
M
N
O

(Continued on next page.)

Case

O (Continued)

WRONG: Ask Joe *who* you think I should see.

RIGHT: Ask Joe *whom* you think I should see.

WRONG: I do not know *who* to invite.

RIGHT: I do not know *whom* to invite.

(See 10N for the subject of the infinitive.)

P USE *WHO, WHICH,* AND *THAT* CORRECTLY WHEN REFERRING TO PERSONS OR THINGS.

Who is used only of people (and sometimes pets).

Which is used only of animals or things.

That is used of animals and things, and sometimes people.

Which is generally used to introduce a nonrestrictive clause.

That is generally used to introduce a restrictive clause.
(See 2J for discussion of restrictive and nonrestrictive clauses.)

EXAMPLES of restrictive and nonrestrictive clauses.

Doctors *who* are concerned about their patients' welfare always prescribe medicine *that* has been tested and approved.
(*who . . . welfare* and *that . . . approved* are restrictive clauses.)
Maria made some turtle soup, *which* I did not like.
(*which . . . like* is a nonrestrictive clause.)

${}^{O}_{P}$**10**

Case

10 Q **USE THE POSSESSIVE CASE WHEN PRONOUNS MODIFY GERUNDS.**

WRONG: Do you mind *him* being here?

RIGHT: Do you mind *his* being here?

WRONG: We did not like *them* borrowing our books.

RIGHT: We did not like *their* borrowing our books.

COMMENT: *His* and *their* in the two examples above are no longer pronouns but possessive adjectives.

NOTE the distinction of *him* and *his* in the examples below.

> I saw *him* gambling at Las Vegas. (*Him* is the direct object of *saw*.)

> CONTRAST TO

> I saw that *his* gambling was foolhardy. (*His* is a possessive adjective modifying the gerund *gambling*.)

10 Q

Case

DIRECTIONS: Copy each sentence below and include the correct
pronouns in parentheses.

1. He is man (who, which, whom) could easily settle the
    argument between (me and you, you and I, you and me).

2. Mr. Crank was a teacher (who, which, whom) did not mind
    (me, my) asking stupid questions.

3. The trouble with (me and you, you and I, you and me) is
    that we cannot decide (who, whom) to vote for.

4. The policeman saw the dog (who, that) stole the soup bone.

5. I knew it was (her, she) (who, whom) the headmaster was
    seeking.

6. Few of (we, us) children can play Monopoly as well as (they,
    them).

7. Tell me (who, whom) you think is more intelligent than (I,
    me).

8. When (me and Peter, Peter and I, Peter and me) saw the mad
    dog, (us, we) boys ran away.

9. (Sada and her, Her and Sada, She and Sada) did not object
    to (them, their) taking a midnight swim.

(Continued on next page.)

Case

10. (Who, Whom) do you think is uglier than you and (me, I)?

11. The coach (who, whom) everyone hated picked on all boys, particularly (me and Ed, Ed and me, Ed and I).

12. The Congressman will be (whoever, whomever) the voters select.

13. I thought (him, he) to be the most objectionable boy (who, which, whom) ever lived.

14. Father always punished my brother more severely than (I, me).

15. The angry teacher gave (him, he) a better grade on the exam than (I, me).

16. The students (who, which) are expected at the luncheon do not include (you and me, you and I, me and you).

17. Painting her house, (which, that) took Pris four weeks to do, was a messy job.

18. Neither (me nor Fran, I nor Fran, Fran nor I) was told (who, whom) our new teacher would be.

19. Girls (who, whom) boys like do not resent popularity.

20. Was it Jane or (her, she) (who, whom) the lifeguard saw drowning?

Agreement

11A A VERB MUST AGREE WITH ITS SUBJECT IN NUMBER.

COMMENT: *Number, person, gender* are three important terms used in this chapter. Learn them.

NUMBER: When only one person or object is named, its *number* is *singular.* When more than one person or object is named, its *number* is *plural.* The term *singular* or *plural* is used to denote number.

Most nouns form the plural by adding *-s* or *-es.*

Examples

Singular	Plural
school	school*s*
bench	bench*es*

Exceptions

child	children
fish	fish

PERSON: Pronouns and verbs change their form or spelling to denote (1) the person or thing speaking (first person), (2) the person or thing spoken *to* (second person), (3) the person or thing spoken *of* (third person).

Examples

	Singular	Plural
First person	*I* love	*we* love
Second person	*you* love	*you* love
Third person	*he, she, it* loves	*they* love

(Continued on next page.)

105

A**11**

Agreement

11 A (Continued)

GENDER: Nouns or pronouns denoting a male person or object are *masculine*. Nouns or pronouns denoting a female person or object are *feminine*. Nouns or pronouns denoting an object without masculine or feminine features are *neute*

Examples

Masculine	*Feminine*	*Neuter*
he	she	it
his	her	its
lion	lioness	fire
waiter	waitress	train
god	goddess	cloud

NOTE: One of the most frequent ways of changing the gender of masculine nouns to the feminine is by adding the suffixes *-ess, -ette*, and sometimes *-ix*. Today there is a derogatory note in feminizing masculine nouns.

Some classes of nouns still tend to follow the Old English regarding gender. For instance:

Masculine		*Feminine*	
the sun	death	spring	liberty
the ocean	love	nature	the earth
time	anger	cities	the moon
day	war	countries	ships

Agreement

SUBJECT – VERB

B **WORDS OR PHRASES BETWEEN SUBJECT AND VERB SELDOM CHANGE THE NUMBER OF THE VERB.**

WRONG: The misbehavior of the girls and boys *were* expected.

RIGHT: The misbehavior of the girls and boys *was* expected.

WRONG: The unfairness of their teachers *are* well known.

RIGHT: The unfairness of their teachers *is* well known.

C **COMPOUND SUBJECTS TAKE A PLURAL VERB.**

EXAMPLES: The Giants and Pygmies *are* locked in eager battle.

Around the corner *were* the bank and the post office.

Here *come* Lanny and Meg with their trombones.

B
C **11**

Agreement

SUBJECT – VERB

11 D THE FOLLOWING WORDS TAKE SINGULAR VERBS: *EACH, EITHER, NEITHER, ONE, EVERY, EVERYONE, EVERYBODY, NO ONE, NOBODY, ANYONE, SOMEONE, SOMEBODY.*

EXAMPLE: Every one of the girls *has* to bring her Red Cross money.

11 E TWO OR MORE SINGULAR SUBJECTS JOINED BY *OR* OR *NOR* TAKE A SINGULAR VERB.

EXAMPLE: Neither Tom nor Jerry *knows* his lesson.

11 F IF ONE SUBJECT IS SINGULAR AND ONE PLURAL, THE VERB TAKES THE *NUMBER* OF THE *NEARER*.

EXAMPLES: Neither Tom nor the other students *know* their lesson.

Neither his parents nor Ted *plays* much tennis.

11 G THE FOLLOWING WORDS MAY TAKE EITHER SINGULAR OR PLURAL VERBS, DEPENDING ON THE CONTEXT: *ALL, ANY, MOST, NONE, SOME.*

RIGHT: None of the boys in the ninth grade *is* mature. (*Not one* ninth grade boy is mature.)

RIGHT: None of the boys in the ninth grade *are* mature. (*No* ninth grade boys are mature.)

11
D
E
F
G

Agreement

SUBJECT – VERB

H THE VERB TAKES THE NUMBER OF ITS SUBJECT. IT DOES NOT AGREE WITH ITS PREDICATE NOUN OR PRONOUN.

WRONG: My chief complaint *are* teachers and girls.

RIGHT: My chief complaint *is* teachers and girls.

I WHEN THE SUBJECT FOLLOWS THE VERB, THE VERB AGREES IN NUMBER, PARTICULARLY WITH *HERE IS, THERE IS,* AND *WHERE IS*.

WRONG: *Where is* the mustard and hot dogs?

RIGHT: *Where are* the mustard and hot dogs?

J WORDS HAVING TO DO WITH FRACTIONS, MEASUREMENT, MONEY, TIME, AND WEIGHT GENERALLY TAKE A SINGULAR VERB.

EXAMPLES: Two years *is* a long time.

Two thirds *constitutes* a majority.

Ten dollars *does* not buy much.

Agreement

11 K A COLLECTIVE NOUN GENERALLY TAKES A SINGULAR VERB, PARTICULARLY WHEN IT IS THOUGHT OF AS A GROUP. SOME NOUNS, PLURAL IN FORM, ALSO TAKE A SINGULAR VERB.

Collective Nouns	*Nouns Plural in Form*
army	mathematics
crowd	economics
faculty	measles
team	news
class	the United States

NOTE: When such collective words as *number, couple, majority,* and *percent* are used, good sense must make the decision. However, the prepositional phrase following such words often determines whether they are singular or plural.

EXAMPLES: A majority of one *is* required.

The great majority of French voters *are* rather frightened by the results of the election.

A large percent of the students *were* happy.

Fifty percent of the money *was* given away.

Agreement

EXERCISE: This exercise includes agreement usage for rules 11A-11K.

DIRECTIONS: Copy each sentence below and include the correct verb in parentheses.

Part I

1. Speaking and writing formal English (requires, require) some intelligence.

2. There (are, is) milk and eggs in the refrigerator.

3. Neither of the teachers (was, were) popular with the new students.

4. Each of the boys (has, have) to report to the gym.

5. Neither the coach nor the players (know, knows) when the game will be played.

6. A major headache of teachers (is, are) lazy students.

7. Either Vera or her sisters (know, knows) when the party will be given.

8. There (goes, go) Mr. and Mrs. Fallon in their new car.

9. The cause of tornadoes (is, are) known.

10. Five hours of my time (was, were) spent in the library.

Part II

Use a dictionary to determine whether the words listed below are singular or plural:

scissors	mumps	measles
trousers	faculty (school)	jury
tactics	politics	linen

111

Agreement

11 L **PRONOUNS AND POSSESSIVE ADJECTIVES MUST AGREE WITH THEIR ANTECEDENTS IN NUMBER, GENDER, AND PERSON.**

COMMENT: The *antecedent* of a pronoun is that word to which the pronoun refers.

EXAMPLES: Every *boy* must bring *his* books.

Boy is the antecedent of *his*.	*His* agrees in
Boy is singular in number.	*number* – singular
Boy is masculine in gender.	*gender* – masculine
Boy is in the third person.	*person* – third

He is a *boy who* is always on time. (*Who* is the relative pronoun referring to its antecedent *boy*.)

Agreement

M *EACH, EVERY, EITHER, NEITHER, ONE, EVERYONE, EVERYBODY, NO ONE, NOBODY, ANYONE, ANYBODY, SOMEONE, SOMEBODY,* **ARE** *SINGULAR,* **AND PRONOUNS AND POSSESSIVE ADJECTIVES MUST AGREE.**

EXAMPLES: *Each one* of the boys will bow to *his* teachers.

If *anyone* arrives, show *him* to the door.

N TWO OR MORE ANTECEDENTS JOINED BY *OR* OR *NOR* ARE CONSIDERED *SINGULAR,* AND PRONOUNS AND POSSESSIVE ADJECTIVES MUST AGREE.

EXAMPLE: *Neither* Lana *nor* Peg has prepared *her* lesson.

COMMENT: When one of the antecedents is singular and one is plural, the possessive adjective will agree with the nearer.

EXAMPLE: Neither the headmaster nor the teachers were aware of *their* responsibility.

O TWO OR MORE ANTECEDENTS JOINED BY *AND* ARE CONSIDERED *PLURAL,* AND PRONOUNS AND POSSESSIVE ADJECTIVES MUST AGREE.

EXAMPLES: Harry and Jim will bring *their* cars.

When Harry and Jim arrive, *they* will show us the way.

M
N
O
11

Agreement

EXERCISE: This exercise includes pronoun-antecedent agreement for rules 11L-11O.

DIRECTIONS: Copy the sentences below and include the correct words in parentheses.

1. Neither General Smythe nor his aides (has, have) the secret plans.

2. Every student in both schools (were, was) asked to bring (their, his) athletic equipment.

3. If no one (are, is) ready, we cannot leave on time.

4. Why (has, have) neither of the babies eaten (their, her) oatmeal?

5. Either Val or her friends (is, are) certain to bring (her, their) beach chairs to the pool.

6. One of the men (is, are) sure to forget to bring (his, their) lunch.

7. Neither Bill's cousins nor his aunt (is, are) expected at the party.

8. One of the women (was, were) told to bring (her, their) gifts.

9. Each of the boys could finish (his, their) homework as quickly as (he, they) wanted.

10. I like dessert. It's delightful when (you, one) (is, are) served a dish (you, he) (like, likes).

Agreement

P **AVOID CARELESS SHIFTS IN PERSON, PARTICULARLY A LAZY *YOU* OR *YOUR*.**

WRONG: I liked having my report praised. It is wonderful when *you* have *your* work appreciated.

RIGHT: I liked having my report praised. It is wonderful when *one* has *his* work appreciated.

Q **AVOID THE CLUMSY *HIS OR HER*.**

CLUMSY: Neither the boy nor the girl will tell *his or her* secret.

RIGHT: Neither the boy nor the girl will tell *the* secret.

NOTE: An easy way to avoid the *his or her* construction is to make the nouns and verbs plural, as in the example below.

CLUMSY: Each student is reponsible for completing *his or her* homework.

RIGHT: Students are responsible for completing *their* homework.

P
Q **11**

Agreement

DIRECTIONS: Copy the sentences below and include the correct words in parentheses.

1. The dedication of doctors and nurses (is, are) appreciated by many patients.

2. On the ground beside the garage (was, were) the wallet and the keys he had lost.

3. One of the more intelligent and able students (were, was) asked to write (their, his) comments.

4. The dinner Heather most disliked (were, was) hot dogs and baked beans.

5. Four years between elections (are, is) a long time for a small percent of candidates who (is, are) eager to run for office.

6. Neither Hilda nor her classmates (is, are) ready to present (her, their) reports in class.

7. If anyone happens to call, tell (him, them) I will return in an hour.

8. Here (is, are) the paper and the books you asked for.

9. There must be someone among the millions of Americans who (are, is) honest enough to return money (they have, he has) stolen.

10. Either Rita or Roseanne (are, is) wise enough to offer (their, her) opinion on the matter.

Correct Use of Verbs

2 USE THE CORRECT TENSE OF THE VERB.

You must know the following terms:

TENSE is a verb form that denotes time — present, past, and future.

(For further explanation, see 12A-12I.)

EXAMPLES: Present: He hits, he is hitting, he does hit.

Past: He hit, he was hitting, he was hit, he has been hitting, he had hit, he had been hitting.

Future: He will hit, he will be hitting, he will have hit, he will have been hitting.

VOICE is a verb form that shows whether the subject acts (active voice) or is acted upon (passive voice).

Examples

Active	Passive
He hits	He is hit
He is hitting	He is being hit
He hit	He was hit
He has hit	He has been hit

MOOD shows the attitude of the speaker toward the action or condition expressed.

The *indicative mood* declares a fact or asks a question.

(Continued on next page.)

12

Correct Use of Verbs

(Continued)

EXAMPLES: Two types of sentences in indicative mood (see also Appendix 1.)

He is hitting the ball. (Declarative sentence)

Does he hit the ball? (Interrogative sentence)

The *imperative mood* commands or orders. The subject is seldom expressed.

EXAMPLES: Hit the ball!

Do not hit the ball.

The *subjunctive mood* denotes what might be rather than what is. It is commonly found in a subordinate clause introduced by *if, as if, as though,* and with verbs of wishing and suggesting.

(For distinctive forms of the subjunctive, see 12R.)

EXAMPLES: If I *were* a bird, I'd fly.

I wish that he *were* here.

We suggest that he *eat* only two meals a day.

TRANSITIVE: A verb is transitive if it takes an object. It may also be conjugated in the passive voice.

EXAMPLES: He hit the ball. (Transitive verb in active voice)

The ball was hit by him. (Transitive verb in passive voice)

Correct Use of Verbs

12 INTRANSITIVE: A verb is intransitive if it does not take an object. It will generally be followed by an adverb phrase and cannot be conjugated in the passive voice.

EXAMPLE: He *dived* into the pool.

(To test the intransitivity of a verb, ask if it can be conjugated in the passive: *He is dived, he was dived, he will be dived.* The conjugation of this verb in the passive strikes one as immediately ridiculous. There is no question that it must be classed as an intransitive verb.)

A **HELPING (auxiliary) VERB** helps form tenses of other verbs.

EXAMPLES: *have* hit, *can* hit, *shall* hit, *must have been* hit

A **LINKING (state-of-being) VERB** binds and closely relates the subject to a predicate (1) noun, (2) pronoun, or (3) adjective.

ALL FORMS OF THE VERB *TO BE* ARE LINKING VERBS.

Some linking verbs are:

appear	grow	smell
become	look	sound
feel	remain	stay
	seem	taste
		turn

Correct Use of Verbs

12

EXERCISE   **Part I.** Exercise on mood and on transitive and intransitive verbs.

DIRECTIONS: Copy and identify the mood of each italicized verb. Also label *vt.* (transitive) or *vi.*(intransitive).

1.   The boy *wanted* a sailboat, but he *was* happy to have a rowboat.

2.   If I *were* you, I *would hit* him back.

3.   *Go* to the store and *buy* some turnips.

4.   *Does* he *like* parsley in his soup? (one verb)

5.   The thief *smashed* the window and *crept* into the kitchen.

6.   If you *were* to help me, I *would be* grateful.

7.   *Take* the bacon and *crumble* it in the salad.

8.   *Is* he sick, or *is* he well?

9.   The teacher *thought* briefly and then *closed* the door.

10.   Heaven *helps* those who *help* themselves.

Correct Use of Verbs

Part II. Exercise on helping verbs and on active/passive voice.

DIRECTIONS: Identify each sentence as "A" (active voice) or "P" (passive voice). Also write the complete verb of each sentence and underline the helping verbs.

1. The baseball team will be departing next Friday.

2. There will be a party in its honor.

3. The teammates have been talking about the party for a long time.

4. It was the manager's idea to have a party.

5. There had been no such celebrations before.

6. The players were all anticipating the party.

7. A room in a hotel had been provided by the manager.

8. The room is presently being used by an athletic club.

9. Milk, cookies, and beer will have been consumed by Friday night.

10. The manager has been working all day on the preparations.

Correct Use of Verbs

12 LEARN HOW THE PRINCIPAL PARTS OF VERBS FORM
THEIR TENSES.

REGULAR VERBS FORM THEIR PRINCIPAL PARTS BY
ADDING *-D, -ED, -T,* OR *-ING* TO THE PRESENT (FIRST
PRINCIPAL PART).

Present	Present Participle	Past	Past Participle
talk	talking	talked	(have) talked
mean	meaning	meant	(have) meant

IRREGULAR VERBS do not follow the rule above. Their principal
parts must be memorized. Use the dictionary.

Present	Present Participle	Past	Past Participle
lie (intransitive)	lying	lay	(have) lain
lay (transitive)	laying	laid	(have) laid

12

Correct Use of Verbs

2 USE THE FOUR PRINCIPAL PARTS AND HELPING VERBS
TO FORM ALL TENSES OF THE VERB.

Principle parts		*Tenses*
Use Present	..........to form	......Present and Future
Use Past	..............to form	......Past
Use Past Participle	.....to form	......Present Perfect, Past Perfect, Future Perfect
Use Present Participle	..to form	......All the Progressive Tenses

A TABULATION OF A REGULAR VERB AND ITS TENSES

ACTIVE

	Regular	*Progressive*	*Emphatic*
Present	uses	is using	does use
Past	used	was using	did use
Future	will use	will be using	———
Pres. Perfect	has used	has been using	———
Past Perfect	had used	had been using	———
Fut. Perfect	will have used	will have been using	———

PASSIVE

	Regular	*Progressive*
Present	is used	is being used
Past	was used	was being used
Future	will be used	———
Pres. Perfect	has been used	———
Past Perfect	had been used	———
Fut. Perfect	will have been used	———

(Continued on next page.)

12

Correct Use of Verbs

12 (Continued)

A TABULATION OF AN IRREGULAR VERB AND ITS TENSES

ACTIVE

	Regular	*Progressive*	*Emphatic*
Present	lays	is laying	does lay
Past	laid	was laying	did lay
Future	will lay	will be laying	———
Pres. Perfect	has laid	has been laying	———
Past Perfect	had laid	had been laying	———
Fut. Perfect	will have laid	will have been laying	———

PASSIVE

	Regular	*Progressive*
Present	is laid	is being laid
Past	was laid	was being laid
Future	will be laid	———
Pres. Perfect	has been laid	———
Past Perfect	had been laid	———
Fut. Perfect	will have been laid	———

NOTE: The *regular present tense* does not mean the action is going on now (at the present moment) but asserts a customary condition.

The *progressive tenses* denote action in the process of taking place in the past, present, or future. There is an element of unbroken continuity about these tenses that anticipates possible interruption.

The *emphatic tenses* are self-explanatory. (See 12 C.)

12

Correct Use of Verbs

2 A THE PRESENT TENSE EXPRESSES GENERAL OR HABITUAL ACTION.

EXAMPLES: I give; he uses; birds lay eggs.

2 B THE PRESENT PROGRESSIVE EXPRESSES ACTION GOING ON NOW.

EXAMPLES: I am giving; he is using; birds are laying eggs.

12 C THE EMPHATIC PRESENT STRESSES ACTION IN THE FACE OF DOUBT OR DENIAL.

EXAMPLES: I do give; he does use.

12 D THE PRESENT PERFECT TENSE EXPRESSES ACTION THAT MAY HAVE BEEN COMPLETED (PERFECTED) BEFORE THE *PRESENT*.

EXAMPLE: I have paid my debt to society.

BUT SOMETIMES THE ACTION MAY NOT HAVE BEEN COMPLETED.

EXAMPLE: I have known Katy for many years.

A
B
C
D
12

Correct Use of Verbs

TENSES

12 E   **THE PAST TENSE EXPRESSES ACTION THAT TOOK PLACE IN THE PAST BUT DID NOT CONTINUE TO THE PRESENT.**

EXAMPLES: I have given; he used; birds laid eggs.

12 F   **THE PAST PROGRESSIVE IS USED *ONLY* TO SHOW ACTION GOING ON IN THE PAST THAT ANTICIPATES INTERRUPTION.**

WRONG: My mother was always nagging me.

RIGHT: As my mother was nagging me, my father entered the room.

12 G   **THE PAST PERFECT TENSE EXPRESSES ACTION COMPLETED IN THE PAST BEFORE SOME OTHER ACTION HAS OCCURRED.** (See also 13H.)

WRONG: If Sally *liked* him, she would have consented to go.

RIGHT: If Sally *had liked* him, she would have consented to go.

WRONG: After I *was* there a week, I decided to depart.

RIGHT: After I *had been* there a week, I decided to depart.

12
E
F
G

Correct Use of Verbs

TENSES

12 H   **THE FUTURE TENSE EXPRESSES ACTION THAT WILL TAKE PLACE SOME TIME IN THE FUTURE.**

         EXAMPLE: He will pay his debts.

12 I   **THE FUTURE PERFECT TENSE EXPRESSES ACTION IN THE FUTURE COMPLETED BEFORE SOME OTHER FUTURE ACTION.**

         EXAMPLE: When Mr. Jones reaches retirement, he *will have been* on the faculty twenty-five years.

H
I **12**

Correct Use of Verbs

CARELESS SHIFTS

12 J AVOID CARELESS SHIFTS IN *TENSE* IN THE SENTENCE, THE PARAGRAPH, THE COMPOSITION.

WRONG: They *stop* at a restaurant, and Amanda *disappeared.*

RIGHT: They *stopped* at a restaurant, and Amanda disappeared.

12 K AVOID CARELESS SHIFTS IN *SUBJECT.*

WRONG: *Bill* studied hard, and his *free time* was little.

RIGHT: *Bill* studied hard and *had* little free time.

12 L AVOID CARELESS SHIFTS IN *VOICE.*

WRONG: The *class* of '74 gave a party, and *it* was decided to invite the eighth grade. (Shift in voice and subject)

RIGHT: The *class* of '74 *gave* a party and *decided* to invite the eighth grade.

WRONG: *Bill* liked his gifts, and *they* were carefully stored. (Shift in voice and subject)

RIGHT: *Bill liked* his gifts and carefully *stored* them.

12   J
   K
   L

Correct Use of Verbs

CARELESS SHIFTS/PASSIVE

2 M AVOID CARELESS SHIFTS IN PERSON AND IN NUMBER.

WRONG: The dictionary is a valuable tool for all students. *You* will find *you* cannot write well without it. (Shift in person)

RIGHT: The dictionary is a valuable tool for all students. *They* will find *they* cannot write well without it.

WRONG: *One* should love *their* neighbors. (Shift in number)

RIGHT: *One* should love *his* neighbors.

2 N USE THE ACTIVE VOICE WHENEVER POSSIBLE. USE THE PASSIVE VOICE SPARINGLY.

WEAK: Your gracious letter was welcomed by all.

STRONGER: All the students welcomed your gracious letter.

NOTE: Do not use active and passive voice in the same sentence.

WRONG: Allie hated driving, but most of the time the car was driven by him.

RIGHT: Allie hated driving, but most of the time he drove the car.

12 O AVOID THE ELIDED PASSIVE.

WEAK: Suddenly a noise was heard. (By whom?)

STILL WEAK: Suddenly a noise was heard by us.

STRONGEST: Suddenly we heard a noise.

M
N
O
12

Correct Use of Verbs

12 O EXERCISE: This exercise includes verb usage
for rules 12N and 12O.

DIRECTIONS: Rewrite the following sentences in the active voice.

1. The ball was dropped by the feeble pitcher.

2. A good time was had by all who went to the party.

3. My composition was graded unfairly by the teacher.

4. It was on a rainy day that I began to cook the cabbage.

5. Your kindness will never be forgotten.

6. There was a fly swimming in my soup.

7. It is discouraging to lose ten games in a row.

8. The eraser was hurled by the angry teacher.

9. The presents were appreciated by all.

10. There are over twenty students seated in the classroom.

For the more advanced students, correct these elided passives. (See 12O.)

11. A new agricultural policy was adopted to alleviate the short-ages.

12. Soon the sun was seen slowly rising over the valley.

13. The medicine was prescribed to help the patient.

14. A definite course of action was decided upon.

15. A new set of procedures was set down to establish uniformity.

Correct Use of Verbs

EXPLETIVES/TRANSITIVE AND INTRANSITIVE

2 P AVOID STARTING SENTENCES WITH LACKLUSTER EXPLETIVES SUCH AS *IT IS, THERE IS, THERE WAS*.

WEAK: *There were* many students who did not come to the dance.

STRONGER: Many students did not come to the dance.

WEAK: *It was* many years before we saw her again.

STRONGER: We did not see her for many years.

2 Q DO NOT USE A TRANSITIVE VERB FOR AN INTRANSITIVE VERB, OR AN INTRANSITIVE VERB FOR A TRANSITIVE VERB.

WRONG: We *exited* the lobby. (*Exit* is not a transitive verb.)

RIGHT: We *exited from* the lobby.

WRONG: He wanted to *proceed* his journey. (*Proceed* is not a transitive verb.)

RIGHT: He wanted to *proceed on* his journey.

WRONG: She tried to *elude from* the police. (*Elude* is a transitive verb.)

RIGHT: She tried to *elude* the police.

P
Q **12**

Correct Use of Verbs

SUBJUNCTIVE

12 R USE THE SUBJUNCTIVE MOOD TO DENOTE WHAT MIGHT BE RATHER THAN WHAT IS.

The subjunctive forms differ from the indicative in only three ways:

(1) *I was* ⎱ becomes ⎰ *I were*
(2) *He, she, it was* ⎱ becomes ⎰ *he, she, it were*

(3) The third person singular of all verbs drops the *s* in the present active subjunctive.

EXAMPLES: If I *were* you, I should obey the teacher.

I wish that he *were* here.

I suggested that he *bring* only his brother.

12 S DO NOT CONFUSE THE VERBS *LIE* AND *LAY*.

Compare the principal parts:

LIE (recline)   lying, lay, (have) lain
LAY (put, set)   laying, laid, (have) laid

LIE is intransitive and almost invariably is followed immediately by a prepositional phrase.

EXAMPLE: She *lay* on the couch (prep. phrase).

LAY is transitive and almost invariably is followed immediately by a direct object.

EXAMPLE: *Lay* the *book* (direct obj.) on the table.

12 **R**
S

Correct Use of Verbs

12 REVIEW EXERCISE

Part I—Verbs. Copy the sentences below and correct the tense or form of the italicized verbs.

1. Arnie hoped that he *was* talented enough to become an opera singer after he *went* to a concert and *heard* Pavarotti sing.

2. Edna and Mae waited until sunset, and then they *leave* the hotel and *take* a taxi to the theater.

3. Next June all students *take* their final exams.

4. Mr. Wence *was* his teacher and *knew* him long before he became famous.

5. Grogan *escaped* prison and *is* loose for three months before the police finally captured him.

6. Margo notices a purse *laying* on the sidewalk and then *picked* it up and *tried* to find the owner.

Part II—Careless Shifts. Copy the sentences below and correct careless shifts in subject, voice, and person and number.

1. The luncheon club voted to have a Christmas dinner, and all the food and the decorations were supplied by the members.

2. Debbie owned three antique cars, and every night they were put away in her garage.

3. Vegetables are healthy for a person on a diet. You should also eat plenty of fruit and yogurt.

4. The class president and vice-president met on Tuesday, and it was decided to have a bake sale at recess the following Friday.

Abusage

13 DO NOT USE LAZY WORDS OR UNGRAMMATICAL DEVICES.

COMMENT: This chapter lists a number of formulas
writers employ lazily or carelessly instead of
selecting the precise word or phrase.

GET   GOT

13 A AVOID THE UNTHINKING USE OF *GET*, EVEN WHEN USED
CORRECTLY IN IDIOMS OR IN ITS BASIC MEANING OF
OBTAIN.

GET/GOT: This fine, strong verb has become such a lazy, repetitious
device in avoiding the concrete word that some instructors
forbid its use except in direct discourse.

Lazy usage: He *got* ten dollars from his father.

Possible alternative: He *received* ten dollars from his father.

Stronger: His father *donated* ten dollars to his cause.

Lazy usage: He *got* out of bed.

Possible alternatives:
>He *slid* out of bed.
>He *bounced* out of bed.
>He *groped* his way out of bed.

More graphic: He threw back the covers and leaped from his cot.

(Continued on next page.)

13 A

Abusage

GET   GOT

Lazy usage: He *got mad.*

Possible alternative: He *became angry.*

More precise: His cheeks flushed, and his eyes flashed. Daddy had lost his temper.

Lazy usage: She *got* married to Bill.

Possible alternative: She *married* Bill.

More precise: Laura Lorenz, a lovely bride, married Bill in a beautiful ceremony.

BRING AND *TAKE*

3 B   **DO NOT CONFUSE** *BRING* **AND** *TAKE*.

BRING has to do with motion *toward* the speaker.

TAKE has to do with motion *away* from the speaker.

WRONG: *Bring* this report to your teacher.

RIGHT: *Take* this report to your teacher.

RIGHT: *Bring* me a tall, cool drink.

Abusage

SLANGY COMPLIMENTARY ADJECTIVES

13 c **DO NOT USE SLANGY *COMPLIMENTARY* ADJECTIVES OR ADVERBS UNLESS THEY STRICTLY APPLY.**

The following are frequently misused:

awesome	fantastically
cool	great
divine	neat
divinely	sharp
fabulous	terrific
fabulously	tough
fantastic	

WRONG: It was a *cool* movie.

RIGHT: It was an *amusing* (*entertaining, delightful*) movie.

BETTER: The fast action, sharp humor, and fine direction make it an entertaining movie.

WRONG: Danny dances *divinely*.

RIGHT: Danny dances *well*.

BETTER: Danny's dancing has rhythm and a fine sense of timing.

Abusage

SLANGY HORROR ADJECTIVES

D **DO NOT USE SLANGY *HORROR* ADJECTIVES OR ADVERBS UNLESS THEY STRICTLY APPLY.**

The following are frequently misused:

awful, awfully	outrageous, outrageously
bad, badly	terrible, terribly
horrible, horribly	tragic, tragically
lousy, lousily	

USE A DICTIONARY TO CHECK THE EXACT MEANING OF THESE WORDS.

WRONG: She made an *awful* mistake.

RIGHT: She made a *serious* mistake.

WRONG: The party last night was *lousy.*

RIGHT: The party last night was *unexciting.*

BETTER: The party last night was *dull, flat, insipid.*

D13

Abusage

SLANGY SIZE ADJECTIVES

13 E **DO NOT USE SLANGY SIZE ADJECTIVES, ADVERBS, OR TRITE OVERSTATEMENTS UNLESS THEY STRICTLY APPLY.**

The following are frequently misused:

all	immensely	really
amazing	incredible	tons of
big	great	too much
enormous	greatly	unbelievable
enormously	huge	very big
immense	millions of	whole

USE A DICTIONARY FOR THE EXACT MEANING OF THESE WORDS.

WRONG: We had a *really great* time.

ON THE WAY: Everyone enjoyed the party.

BETTER: The cool drinks, the soft music, and the beautiful girls made the party a success.

WRONG: Calista was *immensely* popular with the faculty.

ON THE WAY: Calista was *extremely* popular with the faculty.

BETTER: Calista's cheerful industry made her popular with the faculty.

TRITE: I received *tons of* presents at my birthday party.

OVERSTATED: Minnie stayed for a *whole* week and I showed her *all* the shops in town.

BETTER: Minnie stayed for a week, and I showed her *many* of the shops in town.

13 E

Abusage

FUZZY PREPOSITIONS

3 F DO NOT USE PREPOSITIONS FUZZILY TO TAKE THE PLACE OF OTHER PARTS OF SPEECH.

WRONG: My father was *against me* (preposition for verb) having an allowance.

RIGHT: My father was *opposed to my having* an allowance.

WEAK: I was *on* (preposition for verb) Long Lake with my parents.

RIGHT: I was *vacationing* on Long Lake with my parents.
(See also 16A.)

WEAK: Lisa was a beautiful girl *with* (preposition for pronoun and verb) blond hair *to* (preposition for pronoun and verb) her shoulders.

BETTER: Lisa was a beautiful girl *who had* blond hair *that fell* to her shoulders.

F **13**

Abusage

13 G AVOID THE LAZY USE OF *GOOD* AND *BAD*.
(See also 14 B.)

COMMENT: Remember that the basic meaning of *good* and *bad* has to do with right and wrong conduct. Vivid, concrete adjectives can almost invariably be found to take the place of the overworked *good* and *bad*.

WEAK: We had a *good* time.

BETTER: We had an *enjoyable* time.

BETTER YET: Because of the strong punch and rich food, we had a fine time.

WEAK: The food was *bad*.

BETTER: The food was *not well prepared*.

BETTER YET: The food, poorly prepared and unattractively served, did not appeal to us.

RIGHT: Generally the clergy strive to be *good* people.

RIGHT: Because Jim had stolen the money, the police considered him a *bad* boy.

Abusage

HAD

H **USE THE HELPING VERB *HAD* TO SHOW ACTION COMPLETED IN THE PAST.** (See also 12G.)

WRONG: Bill *lost* his wallet, but it did not bother him.

RIGHT: Bill *had lost* his wallet, but it did not bother him.

WRONG: She *was* a governor before becoming a senator.

RIGHT: She *had been* a governor before becoming a senator.

IN/INTO

I **DO NOT CONFUSE *IN* AND *INTO*.**

In is used to show that one is already *inside* a *something*.

Into is used to show that one is going *toward* a *something*. It is generally used with a verb of motion.

WRONG: Scott burst *in* the room.

RIGHT: Scott burst *into* the room.

RIGHT: Scott sailed his boat *in* Greenwich harbor. (Correct: if within the harbor itself.)

**H
I 13**

Abusage

ADJECTIVES, ADVERBS CONFUSED

13 J DISTINGUISH BETWEEN ADJECTIVES AND ADVERBS.

BE ON THE ALERT FOR PREDICATE ADJECTIVES FOLLOWING LINKING (STATE-OF-BEING) VERBS.

EXAMPLE: My dog smells good. (My dog has just had a bath.)

My dog smells well. (My dog is a good hunter.)

Adjectives and adverbs to distinguish:

easy — easily	slow — slowly
good — well	real — really
quick — quickly	bad — badly

WRONG: He catches passes *real good*.

RIGHT: He catches passes *well*.

WRONG: George felt *badly* when his dog died.

RIGHT: George felt *bad* when his dog died.

WRONG: He walked off the floor *dejected*.

RIGHT: He walked off the floor *dejectedly*.

COMPARATIVES, SUPERLATIVES CONFUSED

13 K DISTINGUISH BETWEEN THE COMPARATIVE AND THE SUPERLATIVE DEGREE OF ADJECTIVES.

COMMENT: Use the comparative degree for two persons or things, the superlative for three or more.

WRONG: Was July or August *hottest*?
RIGHT: Was July or August *hotter*?

WRONG: Which is the *best* place to go—Macy's or Saks?

RIGHT: Which is the *better* place to go—Macy's or Saks?

13 J
K

Abusage

A LOT/LOTS

13 L DO NOT USE *A LOT OF, LOTS OF* FOR *MUCH, MANY, A GREAT DEAL.*

NOTE: *Alot* is the misspelling of *a lot.*
A *lot* can also be a measurement of land.

WEAK: My grandfather has *a lot of* money.

BETTER: My grandfather has a *good deal* of money.

BETTER
YET: My grandfather is *extremely* wealthy, owning many
apartment houses in the city.

DANGLING MODIFIERS

3 M **REWRITE SENTENCES THAT USE ANY TYPE OF DANGLING MODIFIERS.**
(See also 20E.)

WRONG: *Undefeated in twelve games,* it looked like a certain winning season for the football team. (*Undefeated in twelve games* could here only modify *it.*)

RIGHT: *Undefeated in twelve games,* the football team was certain of having a winning season.

WRONG: *After watching the sunset,* the moon rose in solemn splendor. (Did the moon watch the sunset?)

RIGHT: *After we had watched the sunset,* the moon rose in solemn splendor.

Abusage

13 N **AVOID USING *NICE* TO MEAN *AGREEABLE, PLEASING, ATTRACTIVE, FRIENDLY, KIND.***
(See also 14B.)

Nice, in formal writing, should be used to mean *precise, showing discrimination.*

RIGHT: Dr. White's laboratory experience demonstrated a *nice* technique.

RIGHT: Harry showed *nice* discrimination in his choice of words.

WEAK: Griff is a *nice* fellow.

BETTER: Griff was well-mannered, gracious, and considerate of others.

WEAK: It was a *nice* party.

BETTER: The hot food, the cool drinks, and the pretty girls made the party a success.

Abusage

O DO NOT USE *AND, AND SO, AND ALSO, AND THEN, THEN* LOOSELY TO JOIN UNRELATED INDEPENDENT CLAUSES. (See also 22C.)

STRINGY: The day was hot, *and (so)* I decided not to attend.

Stringy, loose sentences of this type can often be easily corrected by using subordinate clauses.

BETTER: Because the day was hot, I decided not to attend.

CHOPPY USE: Hortense had cleaned up her room. *Then* she dashed downstairs to eat breakfast. She ate her cereal. *Then* she decided to visit her friend Chunky next door. *Then* they decided to ride to the Bruce Museum.

The choppy, repetitious *then* can often be easily corrected by (1) using subordinate clauses or (2) using other connectives such as:

afterwards	besides	furthermore
again	but	next
at last	however	still
at the same time	finally	soon

IMPROVED: After Hortense had cleaned up her room (subordinate clause), she dashed downstairs to breakfast. She ate her cereal. *Then* (correctly used here) she decided to visit her friend Chunky next door. They rode their bicycles for a while. Finally (*at last, afterwards*) they decided to ride to the Bruce Museum.

O13

Abusage

13 P AVOID USING *PEOPLE, PERSON, THEY,* AND OTHER SUCH IMPERSONAL NOUNS AND PRONOUNS.

WEAK: The sergeant glared at the *people* in front of him.

BETTER: The sergeant glared at the *new recruits* in front of him.

WEAK: *People* say a new highway will cut through town.

BETTER: I have heard *rumors* that a new highway will cut through town.

WEAK: Sal saw him speaking to a strange *person.*

BETTER: Sal saw him speaking to a *tall, thin, strange man.*

WEAK: *They* say it will rain tomorrow.

BETTER: The *Daily News* predicts rain for tomorrow.

Abusage

3 Q DO NOT USE THE PREPOSITION *LIKE* FOR THE CONJUNCTION *AS, AS IF, AS THOUGH.*

WRONG: If you like spaghetti *like* I do, you should rush right out and buy some.

RIGHT: If you like spaghetti *as* I do, you should rush right out and buy some.

WRONG: They screamed *like* the world *was* coming to an end.

RIGHT: They screamed *as if (as though)* the world *were* coming to an end. (See 12R.)

WRONG: *Like* I said, . . .

RIGHT: *As* I was saying, . . .

WRONG: Tell it *like* it is.

RIGHT: State the facts.

                Tell the truth.

Q **13**

Abusage

LONG, ROUNDABOUT CONSTRUCTIONS

13 R DO *NOT* USE LONG, ROUNDABOUT CONSTRUCTIONS TO BEGIN YOUR COMPOSITION OR TO RESTATE THE TASK ASSIGNED.

The following devices are frequently used:

WRONG: In my composition I am going to tell you about my trip to Paris.

WRONG: This composition is all about my trip to Paris.

WRONG: This book report is on *Call of the Wild.*

RIGHT: The last time I was in Paris, . . .

RIGHT: Last summer I met a fascinating man in Paris who . . .

RIGHT: The novel *Call of the Wild* took place in . . .

SO

13 S AVOID USING *SO:*
1) AS A CONJUNCTIVE ADVERB, EVEN IF PUNCTUATED CORRECTLY.
2) IN AN EXCLAMATORY SENSE OR FOR EMPHASIS.
3) TO BEGIN A SENTENCE.

So has become a lazy linking device and tends to make the sentence in which it is used long and stringy. Introducing the sentence with a subordinate clause makes a far more effective sentence. (See also 1G.)

STRINGY: The teachers and students had arrived early; *so* they decided to tour the art galleries.

IMPROVED: Because the teachers and students had arrived early, they decided to tour the art galleries.

(Continued on next page.)

Abusage

SO

Further comments on the uses of *so:*

The *so* discussed on the previous page has been used as a conjunctive adverb meaning *therefore, for this reason, as a consequence.*

AVOID *using **so** in an exclamatory sense or for emphasis.*

WRONG: He is *so* divine!

WRONG: The food here is *so* good.

AVOID *using **so** to start a sentence.*

WRONG: Mom and Dad were angry. *So* they would not let me have the car.

There are other uses of *so.* Do not confuse them with the conjunctive adverb. Be sure to punctuate correctly.

***So** as an adverb* requires no punctuation.

EXAMPLE: Katie was *so* beautiful that the boys were afraid of her.

***So that** as a subordinating conjunction* requires no punctuation.

EXAMPLE: Bill lied to his father *so that* he might avoid a whipping.

s 13

Abusage

13 T **AVOID THE VAGUE USE OF *THING* OR ANY COMBINATION OF *THING* SUCH AS *SOMETHING, ANYTHING.* BE PRECISE. NAME THE *THING* OR *THINGS.***

VAGUE:	Many *things* have happened to Gertrude.
MORE PRECISE:	Gertude suffered loss of money, loss of hearing, and loss of a husband.
VAGUE:	I have *nothing* to do today.
MORE PRECISE:	The sailing has been called off; I haven't enough money to go bowling; my friends have all left town. In short I am bored.
VAGUE:	My shopping list consists of many *things.*
MORE PRECISE:	On my shopping list were soap, eggs, and puppy biscuits.
VAGUE:	The Rosickys had *everything* with no money.
MORE PRECISE:	The Rosickys enjoyed happiness despite having no money.

13 T

Abusage

13 U AVOID VAGUE REFERENCE OF *THIS* USED EITHER AS AN ADJECTIVE OR AS A PRONOUN.
(See also 19C.)

VAGUE: I did not like *this* in the book.

STRONGER: I did not like the author's attempt at humor in the book.

VAGUE: I did not like *this* book.

STRONGER: I did not like the novel *Nightwatch*.

VAGUE: There was *this* girl whom we liked for her gentleness.

STRONGER: We liked *Martha* for her gentleness.

WEAK VERBS: *DO, GO, COME, WALK*

13 V AVOID THE WEAK COLORLESS VERBS *DO, GO, COME, WALK*.
(See also 14B.)

WEAK: I *did* a great many things last weekend.

STRONGER: I *sailed, bowled,* and *played tennis* last weekend.

WEAK: The headmaster *walked* down the corridor and *went* into the study hall.

STRONGER: The headmaster *strode* down the corridor and *burst* into the study hall.

WEAK: The boat *came* into the harbor.

STRONGER: The boat *steamed* (*sailed, tacked*) into the harbor.

U
V **13**

Abusage

13 w DO NOT USE CONSTRUCTIONS SUCH AS *IS WHEN, IS BECAUSE,* AND *LIKE WHEN.*

COMMENT: *Is* and *was* are linking verbs and cannot be followed immediately by adverb clauses beginning with *when, because,* and *where.* They must, instead, be followed by predicate nominatives.

WRONG: My worst defeat *was when* my sister beat me at poker.

TO CORRECT: Use *occur* or *take place* instead of the verb *is* or *was.*

RIGHT: My worst defeat *occurred* (*took place*) when my sister beat me at poker.

WRONG: The reason the United States is powerful *is because* it is wealthy.

TO CORRECT: Use *that* for *because,* or recast the sentence.

RIGHT: The reason the United States is powerful is that it is wealthy. (Or: The United States is powerful because it is wealthy.)

WRONG: Ollie does stupid things *like when* he ate the paint.

COMMENT: *Like* as a preposition must be followed by a noun or pronoun — not an adverb clause.

RIGHT: Ollie does stupid things like eating paint.

13 w

Abusage

13 x SPELLING: [IN CORRECTIONS, WRITE EACH WORD TEN TIMES IN CONTEXT.]

ACCEPT this gift/ everyone EXCEPT me
A LOT (never *alot*)
ALL READY to leave/he had ALREADY gone
ALL RIGHT (never *alright*)
ARE you well?/come to OUR house
BELIEVE it or not
DOCTOR (not -ER)
DOES he like candy? (never *dose*)
ESCAPE (not *excape*)
FRIEND
GRAMMAR (not -ER)
HEAR with your *ear*/HERE is not *there*
HOLE in one's head/the WHOLE thing
IT'S (it is) raining/the team and ITS coach
KNOW the answers/NO way out
LOSE the game/LOOSE as a goose
NEW shoes/she KNEW the answer
OF mice and men/OFF to the races
OF the school/could HAVE (not *of*) gone
PAST is not present/he PASSED the gravy
RECEIVE a letter
SUPPOSE*D* TO (with the *D*)
THEN what happened?/bigger THAN I am
THERE he is/THEY'RE (they are) smart/THEIR books
THREW a pitch/THROUGH the tunnel/THROW a ball
TO go TO bed/TOO hard for me/TWO dollars
USE*D* TO (with the *D*)
WEAR warm clothes/WHERE are you?
WEATHER forecasting/I don't know WHETHER to go
WE'RE (we are) leaving/we WERE going
WHICH one? (not *wich* or *witch*)
WHOSE book is this?/WHO'S (who is) the captain?
WITH (not *whith*)
WOMAN (only one)/WOMEN (more than one)
WON a prize/ONE dollar
WRITE a letter/my RIGHT hand
WRITING a letter/a WRITTEN report
YOUR books/YOU'RE (you are) welcome

x13

13 x   [WORDS I FREQUENTLY MISSPELL]

_____ _____

_____ _____

_____ _____

_____ _____

_____ _____

_____ _____

_____ _____

_____ _____

_____ _____

_____ _____

13 x

Abusage

3 y DO NOT USE *YOU* IMPERSONALLY AS IF REFERRING TO ANY READER, OR TO MANKIND IN GENERAL.
(See also 19D.)

WRONG: Jerome was angry, and *you* would be too, if *your* boots had been stolen. (Change of person. See 12M.)

WRONG: If *you* want action, here is a book *you* should read. (Too general)

WRONG: As *you* can see, General Arnold turned into a traitor. (Too general)

Generally the best way to avoid such usage is to use the third person.

RIGHT: Jerome was angry, as *anyone* would have been, if *his* boots had been stolen.

RIGHT: If *readers* want action, here is a book *they* should read.

RIGHT: The *author* makes it quite clear why General Arnold became a traitor.

Y **13**

Abusage

PRECISE MEANING

13 z USE A WORD WITH PRECISE REGARD TO ITS BASIC MEANING.

Examples of words used in slipshod fashion and particularly where the writer has substituted sound for meaning:

> *Then/now:* The day of the race was cold, and *now* I was ready to start.

> *Tangled/mingled:* I rushed into the *mingled* branches of the bushes.

Other examples of words used in slipshod fashion where sentences need to be recast:

> How did you *killed* him?

> He attacked the group of *Paris* soldiers.

> I cast my line into the *hopeful* fishing hole.

> I feel that the mountains have no real *descriptive.*

> The starlet was admired for her *fulsome* charms.

USE YOUR DICTIONARY.

13 z

Abusage

13 DIRECTIONS: Rewrite the sentences below to correct the abusage of the italicized words.

1. Isaac *got up* in a hurry, *got* his clothes on, *got* downstairs quickly, and *went in* the kitchen and *got* a hurried breakfast so that he could *get* the bus on time.

2. The science fiction movie was *so* thrilling! It made *you* think *you* were really on *your* way to Mars.

3. The reason Marnie did *good* at school *is because* she began to study harder *like* her father *suggested*.

4. Although the weather was *lousy*, Gay had a *fantastic* time in the kitchen baking *tons of* cookies for her *terrific* boy friend.

5. Mr. Potts had not *gotten anything* for his wife's birthday, and *this* troubled him, *so* he decided to *bring* his wife to a *nice* movie.

6. Elmo had *lots of* friends, but *people* said he acted *like* the *whole* human race *was against him.*

7. Deedee was *real* diligent *like when* she stayed up until 2 a.m. finishing the *things* she had to *do* for her history project.

8. *Looking around the showroom,* the furniture looked *good, and so* Inga thought she might *bring* home a new lamp.

9. *They* say Oscar never *tried* hard at school and never *minded* his *bad* grades until he *got* a *good* teacher.

10. Is *a lot of* candy or some *nice* stationery the *best* present for a birthday?

Choice of Word

PRECISION

14 **CHOOSE WORDS THAT ARE VIVID AND FRESH.**
(See also 13Z.)

COMMENT: Some principles for the choice of words:

1. Choose the concrete word rather than the abstract.

2. Choose the familiar word rather than the far-fetched.

3. Choose the single word rather than the roundabout construction.

4. Choose the short word rather than the long.

5. Choose the Anglo-Saxon word rather than the word derived from the Latin (e.g., use *stingy* rather than *parsimonious*).

6. Choose the strong active verb rather than the weak passive verb.

14

Choice of Word

14 A   USE CONCRETE RATHER THAN ABSTRACT NOUNS.

COMMENT: *Concrete nouns* can be felt, smelled, touched, seen, or heard.

EXAMPLES: *hut, gun, mother, carving knife*

COMMENT: *Abstract nouns* name qualities, ideas, characteristics. Such qualities cannot be felt, smelled, touched, seen, or heard.

EXAMPLES: *loveliness, strength, courage, truth*

ABSTRACT: She had become a girl of great *beauty.*

CONCRETE: Her dark hair, milk-white complexion, and sparkling blue eyes had turned her into a beautiful girl.

ABSTRACT: The headmaster spoke about school *spirit* and *that sort of thing.*

CONCRETE: Mr. Webster, the headmaster, spoke to the students about cheering the team on to victory.

(Continued on next page.)

A 14

Choice of Word

14 A (Continued)

ABSTRACT: Dave's appearance was not everything that could be desired.

CONCRETE: Dave's uncombed hair, baggy pants, and dirty fingernails did not impress his teachers.

ABSTRACT: We were surrounded by darkness, and we were frightened.

CONCRETE: The inky blackness of the night frightened us.

Choice of Word

14 B CHOOSE WORDS THAT ARE VIVID AND FRESH RATHER THAN
WORDS THAT ARE WORN OUT AND COLORLESS.
(See also 13V.)

A thesaurus is extremely useful here.

Some COLORLESS words: Some ALTERNATIVES:

bad..................   inferior, harmful, evil, wicked, tainted,
                                   ill, vile, stingy, corrupt, cruel

come ....   draw near, reach, advance, close in,
                                   arrive, drive, go ahead, show up

do...................   accomplish, complete, conclude,
                                   produce, act, finish, carry out,
                                   perform, behave, cause

easy ....   simple, uncomplicated, facile, gradual,
                                   slack, comfortable, smooth,
                                   manageable, slight, plain

get on a horse..........   mount, climb on, scramble, leap,
                                   jump, vault

go....................   leave, travel, proceed, reach, pass,
                                   trudge, strut, stride, saunter,
                                   stroll, depart

good ....   useful, expert, skillful, moral,
                                   upright, honorable, kind, proper,
                                   loyal, safe, well-behaved, obedient,
                                   genuine, careful, fresh, favorable,
                                   savory, excellent, skilled, just, warm,
                                   reliable, satisfying, enjoyable

(Continued on next page.)

B 14

Choice of Word

14 B (Continued)

Some COLORLESS words: Some ALTERNATIVES:

hard .... arduous, troublesome, tough, stubborn,
harsh, difficult, rigid, strong,
callous, cruel

move .... creep, crawl, sidle, inch, sneak, glide,
drift, pass, flow, march, travel, proceed

nice .... agreeable, attractive, lively,
comfortable, enjoyable, delightful,
charming, gracious, courteous, cheerful,
friendly, well-mannered, pleasant

say .... tell, speak, relate, state, announce,
declare, assert, answer, whisper,
roar, shout, hiss, mutter, reply

take .... seize, steal, conquer, carry

walk .... swagger, stride, step, pace, march,
tread, hike, wander, tramp, roam,
amble, stagger, trudge, stroll, sidle, creep

work .... labor, toil, exert (oneself), struggle,
strive, achieve, operate, clean,
dig, plow, polish, strain

14 B

Choice of Word

DIRECTIONS: Copy and revise the sentences below and use precise words in place of the italicized words.

1. Louis *got mad* when his father *said,* "You are *bad.*"

2. Amanda was admired for her *beauty.*

3. Mrs. Peale *said to* her friend, "That dinner was *good.*"

4. Sarah had many *things to do* before dinner.

5. Mr. French *worked* all day, and then he *walked* home.

6. The counselor *told* a *scary* story.

7. Mrs. Chud was *nice,* but Mr. Chud was *mean.*

8. Lou *walked* out of the house to *go* to the *store.*

9. Willie *went to* a new school and *said* the work was *hard.*

10. Because of the *things* Paul and I *did* on our *trip,* we had a *good* time.

11. Thoreau liked to live *surrounded by nature.*

12. When my family and I *went* to Vermont, we *took* our *equipment.*

13. Anne was not only *good-looking* but also *nice.*

14. Gus found it *easy* to *get* the train to New York.

15. The old car *moved* down the road and finally *came to* a gas station.

163

EX B 14

Choice of Word

14 C **CHOOSE PHRASES THAT ARE VIVID AND FRESH RATHER THAN CLICHÉS.**

A *cliché* is an expression or idea that has become stale and worn out.

A SHORT LIST OF CLICHÉS

a fate worse than death
a good time was had by all
accidents will happen
all of a sudden
avoid like the plague
better late than never
big as a house
busy as a bee
calm before the storm
dead as a doornail
dull as dishwater
each and every
easier said than done
fat as a pig

few and far between
flat as a pancake
in this day and age
last but not least
make a long story short
method in his madness
once upon a time
pale as death
quick as a cat
quite a few
sick as a dog
slow as molasses
slow but sure
smart as a whip
sweet as a rose

Space is left here so that the teacher may add phrases of more recent coinage to the list.

_____ _____

_____ _____

_____ _____

_____ _____

Choice of Word

D **CHOOSE WORDS THAT ARE VIVID AND FRESH RATHER THAN SLANGY OR INFORMAL.**

COMMENT:　An up-to-date college dictionary gives information on such words. Use it.

A SHORT LIST OF SLANGY, INFORMAL WORDS

awesome	dumbbell	idiot	rap (session)
ball (to have a)	dump (as verb)	jazz	rip-off
blast	far out	jerk	scary
broke	fink	jock	sharp
bug (as verb)	foxy	kid (verb	spaz
bummer	fun (as adj.)	and noun)	stud
chicken (out)	funky	lousy	tough (meaning
cool	goof	mean	excellent)
corny	great	neat	up-tight
crazy	groovy	nuts	way out
creep(y)	gross	off the wall	wicked
cuckoo	guy	out of sight	wimp
cute	hang-up	pig out	wise (guy)
dip	hot (meaning	psyched	-wise (as a suffix)
dude	excellent)	reject (noun)	

Space is left here so that the teacher may add slang of more recent coinage to the list.

_____   _____

_____   _____

_____   _____

D 14

Choice of Word

14 E   USE THE PROPER PREPOSITIONS IN IDIOMS.

COMMENT: An *idiom* is a short expression peculiar to its own language, which generally cannot be analyzed grammatically. There is often only a fine line distinguishing slang and idioms. An accurate, discerning ear is required. When in doubt, consult a dictionary.

Here are a few examples of commonly used idioms:

fair and square	next door to
free and easy	to split hairs
to put up with	to strike a bargain

Many errors of idiom are found in the use of prepositions.

SOME IDIOMATIC PREPOSITIONS

accompanied *with* (things); *by* (people)
accused *of* (not *with*)
addicted *to*
agree *to* (suggestions)
agree *with* (people)
angry *at* (things); angry *with* (people)
frightened *by* (not *of*)
privilege *of* (not *to*)
up—unnecessary use of:
    Wrong: drank *up* the juice
    Wrong: divide *up* the pie
blame *for,* Do not use *blame on*
    Wrong: We blamed the accident *on* Jim.
    Right: We blamed Jim *for* the accident.
compare *to* (*one* person or thing to another)
compare *with* (*two* persons or things to another)

(Continued on next page.)

Choice of Word

SOME IDIOMATIC PREPOSITIONS

die *of* (not *with*)
differ *from* (dissimilarity)
differ *with* (disagreement)
different *from* (with a phrase)
different *than* (with a clause)
wait *on* (service)
wait *for* (arrival of)

Choice of Word

MIXED FIGURES OF SPEECH

14 F   AVOID MIXED FIGURES OF SPEECH.

COMMENT: *Mixed figures of speech* are found primarily in similes and metaphors.

EXAMPLES: *Mixed metaphor:* The President has backed him *to the hilt* (sword play) every time the *chips were down* (poker).

Direct: The President has backed him in every crisis.

Mixed metaphor: The *ship of state* (a boat) has *crucified itself* (torture of an individual) *at the crossroads* (having to do with roads) in this crisis.

Direct: The government has destroyed itself at this critical moment.

Mixed metaphor: The hand that rocked the cradle has kicked the bucket! (Can a hand *kick*?)

Direct: Mother died!

Mixed metaphor: Why did I stick my neck out on a limb for him?

Direct: Why did I take risks for him?

Choice of Word

4 G AVOID NEOLOGISMS.

COMMENT: A *neologism* [Gk. *neo* (new) + *logos* (word)] is here considered as a word that has been changed from one part of speech to another and that has not yet been accepted in formal writing. Advertising men are particularly fond of neologising.

WRONG: Our cigarette *gentles* [sic] the smoke on the way to your throat. (*Gentle* is not accepted as a verb in this sense.)

WRONG: We will have a *fun* day. (*Fun* is not accepted as an adjective.)

WRONG: We *trick-or-treated* on Halloween. (*Trick-or-treated* is not accepted as a verb.)

WRONG: *Sales-wise,* the company was not successful.

When in doubt, consult the dictionary.

G 14

Choice of Word

MALAPROPISMS

14 H AVOID MALAPROPISMS.

COMMENT: A *malapropism* is the unintentional use of one word that sounds like another. The result is often humorous.

WRONG: After *pervading* a questionnaire for the class, Inga conducted a survey.

RIGHT: After *providing* a questionnaire for the class, Inga conducted a survey.

WRONG: Following the operation, the patient was placed in *expensive* care.

RIGHT: Following the operation, the patient was placed in *intensive* care.

14 I   AVOID JARGON.

COMMENT: *Jargon* is the use of meaningless terms or of technical language used by specialists. Strive for straight-forward writing.

WRONG: I would appreciate your *meaningful input* on this matter.

RIGHT: I would appreciate your *thoughtful suggestions* on this matter.

WRONG: Kino had a poor *life style*.

RIGHT: Kino *lived in poverty*.

14 H
I

Choice of Word

DIRECTIONS: Copy and revise the sentences below and replace
italicized words with fresh, vivid language.

1. *To make a long story short,* my father is *as smart as a whip,*
   but he *really bugs me.*

2. When he found himself *in a tight spot,* Hal *put his
   shoulder to the wheel* and *delivered the knockout punch.*

3. Darcy was *enthused* when she learned she had won ten pounds
   of *cold* slaw *for free.*

4. *Quick as a flash,* Helga drank *up* her tea and ran out
   the door *like a frightened rabbit.*

5. Wendy was a *dumbbell* compared *with* her brother Mac,
   as she proved by *goofing* all five of her exams.

6. The huge tackle, *strong as an ox,* was able to
   shoulder-pad the guard out of the way.

7. *Like a bolt from the blue,* the tornado *went* through
   the town and *frighted* the townspeople.

8. Joey became angry *at* his mother because she *put the
   blame on him* for *ripping off* the cookies.

9. Walton was an *expertise* outdoorsman who was addicted *of*
   fishing and who practiced casting his line into the *crick*
   every day.

10. The *guy* thought the *kid* next door was a *jerk,* but
    he believed the *kid's* father was a *cool dude.*

11. Emma had a *healthful* outlook on life until her father
    kicked the bucket, and then she *went bananas.*

12. The *extinguished* speaker *rapped about* those *senior
    citizens* in our town who were *underprivileged.*

EX I **14**

Choice of Word

GLOSSARY OF USAGE

This glossary contains misused words and expressions not found in Chapter 13. Some of these words and expressions demand that you learn to distinguish between them; others have to do with lazy usage. They are not permitted in formal writing.

A, AN. Use *an* before words beginning with a vowel sound: *an* orange; *an* honest man.

A, AN, THE. *A, AN* have a generalizing force. *THE* is used to particularize. *A* warm shower moistened *the* grass.

AFFECT, EFFECT. Distinguish between. *Affect* can only be a verb, meaning *to influence* or *pretend. Effect* as a noun means *result*; as a verb, *to bring about, cause.*

AGGRAVATE. Does *not* mean to *irritate* or to *annoy* a *person.* It means *to make worse,* such as an illness or *situation*: He *aggravated* his illness by taking a cold dip.

ALLUSION, ILLUSION. *Allusion* means *hint, reference*; *illusion* means *misleading image* or *idea.*

ALL OF A SUDDEN. Write *suddenly* instead.

ALMOST. See *MOST.*

ALREADY, ALL READY. The adverb *already* means *before this time.* The pronoun *all* and the adjective *ready* mean that *everyone was ready.*

ALRIGHT. Always a misspelling. Use *all right.*

ALSO. Do not use as a conjunction as in: We visited our relatives. *Also* we saw their animals.

Choice of Word

GLOSSARY OF USAGE

AMONG, BETWEEN. *Among* refers to more than two; *between* literally refers to only two. We divided the booty *among* the boys. We divided the booty *between* Jim and Sally.

AMOUNT, NUMBER. *Amount* refers broadly to quantity; *number* refers to countable objects. The *amount* of sugar; the *number* of men.

(AND) &. Do not use this symbol for *and*. Exception: when part of a company name (the A&P).

APT, LIKELY, LIABLE. *Apt* suggests aptitude for. He is an *apt* disciple. *Liable* suggests chance, risk, danger. He is *liable* to be killed. *Likely* suggests *probability*. We are *likely* to have rain.

AND ALSO. Do not add the *also* in such series as: We bought gum, shoes, *and also* flowers.

AND ETC. Use *etc.* by itself if you must. Do not tack on *and* to the abbreviation *etc.*

BADLY. Do not use to mean *very much* with verbs *want or need*. Wrong: He wanted to leave *badly*. Better: He *very much* wanted to leave.

BEING. The auxiliary participle is often unnecessary. Remove it. (Being) distressed at her sorrow, he offered help.

BEING AS, BEING THAT. Do *not* use for *because, since.* Wrong: *Being that* you are my friend, I will ask your help. Right: *Because* you are my friend, I will ask your help.

BETWEEN, AMONG. See *AMONG.*

J 14

Choice of Word

GLOSSARY OF USAGE

BLACK.   Never capitalize *blacks* referring to Negroes. Always capitalize *Negro*.

BUNCH.   Does not mean *several, a group*. Wrong: A *bunch* of the boys and I. Right: *Several* of the boys and I.

CAN, MAY. *Can* suggests ability. *May* suggests permission or possibility. You *can* do it. You *may* not go.

CLAIM.   *Claim* means *demand, assert ownership of*. It does not mean *say, state, maintain*. Wrong: The boy *claimed* that he had not been there. Right: I *claimed* ownership of the house.

COMP.   Do *not* use for *composition*.

COUPLE. Do not use for *a few, several*. Be specific.

CREEP. The principal parts are *creep, creeping, crept*, not *CREEPED*.

CROWD. Informal for *a set, clique*. Do not use.

DIFFERENT KINDS. A redundancy. *Kind* implies difference. We had three (different) *kinds* of drinks.

Choice of Word

GLOSSARY OF USAGE

DIFFERENT FROM, DIFFERENT THAN. *From* introduces a phrase; *than* introduces a clause (often elliptical). Right: He is *different from* me. Right: The school is *different than* it was ten years ago.

DONE. Do not use for *finished.* Wrong: Are you *done* eating?

DUE TO. Do not use for *because of.*

EFFECT. See *AFFECT.*

e.g./i.e. Do not confuse; *e.g.* means *for example* (Latin, *exempli gratia*); *i.e.* means *namely, that is* (Latin, *id est*). He is fond of sweets, *e.g.,* candy, cakes, and pies. There are four humors, *i.e.,* black bile, yellow bile, phlegm, and blood.

EMIGRATE, IMMIGRATE. *Emigrate* means to go *out of* a place to another. *Immigrate* means to come *into* a place from another.

ETC. Use this abbreviation only when absolutely necessary.

EXCELLENT. Do not qualify as in *very* excellent, *quite* excellent (see also UNIQUE).

FARTHER, FURTHER. *Farther* has to do with measurable physical distance. *Further* has to do with qualities of time or degree, which cannot be measured. Right: He walked *farther* into the woods. Right: We will consider the problem *further* in the future.

J14

Choice of Word

FAZE.   Do not use for *worry*.

FEEL LIKE. Do not use for *believe that*. Wrong: I *feel like* he is mistaken.

FIGURE (v.). Do not use for *think, suppose*. Wrong: I *figured* she was deaf.

FIRST, SECOND, THIRD, etc., is preferred to *firstly, secondly, thirdly*.

FIX.   Do not use informally for a *predicament* or *to punish*. Not acceptable: to be in a *fix*, to *fix* him. Choose exact words.

FUN.   (See 14G.) Do not use as an adjective, as in "a *fun* time." It cannot be compared as adjectives: *fun, funner, funnest*.

FUNNY.   Overused for *peculiar, queer, odd*.

GOOD, WELL. *Good* is an adjective; *well* is an adverb. See 13G for use of *good*.

GUESS.   Do not use for *suppose, think, surmise*. Weak: I *guess* I did well on the test.

GUY.   Do not use for *man, boy, fellow*.

HANGED, HUNG. People are *hanged*; things are *hung*. Right: The stockings *were hung*. Santa Claus *was hanged*.

i.e.   See *e.g.*

ILLUSION. See *ALLUSION*.

IMMIGRATE. See *EMIGRATE*.

Choice of Word

J

IMPLY, INFER. Generally *imply* means that the author or speaker *suggests* or *hints*. *Infer* means that the listener comes to a conclusion by some kind of emotional or thought process. Right: The speaker *implied* that all politicians were dishonest, from which I *inferred* that he felt that Mayor Jones was taking bribes.

INDIAN. Always capitalize.

KID (n.). Do not use for *child* or *student*.

KID (v.). Do not use for *tease* or *ridicule*.

KIND OF, SORT OF. Do not use for *rather, somewhat, a little.* Wrong: He was *kind of* nice but *sort of* overweight.

KIND OF A. *A* is unnecessary. What kind of (a) dog is that?

LEAP.   Principal parts are LEAPED, LEAPING, LEAPT. Do not misspell as *lept*.

LEAVE, LET. *Let* means *allow* or *permit. Leave* means to *depart from.* Wrong: *Leave* me work it out by myself. Right: *Let* me work it out myself. The idiom, *Leave me alone,* is acceptable.

LIABLE. See *APT.*

LIKELY. See *APT.*

-LOOKING. Do not use as suffix, as in funny-*looking* hat; fat-*looking* man; oval-*looking* egg.

J14

Choice of Word

GLOSSARY OF USAGE

MAD.   Do not use for *angry*. It means *insane, crazy.*

MADE, MAKE OUT. Overused. Do not use in the sense of *have it made*: he *made* the train; how did you *make out?* Use such words as *succeed, catch, do well.*

MAKE UP. Do not use in the sense of *make up* one's mind. Use *decide, conclude.*

MATH.   Informal for *mathematics.* Use with care.

MAY.   See *CAN.*

MEAN.   Do not use for *nasty, ill-tempered.* My mother is *mean* suggests that she is (1) miserly, (2) shabby in appearance, (3) of low birth.

MEET UP WITH. Use MEET alone. Wrong: Rae will *meet up with* you in London. Right: Rae will *meet* you in London. MEET WITH means *to confer.* Right: The teacher will *meet with* the students.

MESS.   Do not use referring to *confused, deranged* individuals.

MOST, ALMOST. Do not confuse the superlative of adjective *much* or *many* with the adverb *almost. Most* is not a shortened form of *almost. Most* men, *most* food, but *almost* on time, *almost* there.

MR.   Its plural is MESSRS.

Choice of Word

GLOSSARY OF USAGE

MYSELF. Avoid using the reflective pronoun *myself* instead of *I* and *me.* Examples: My parents and *I* (not *myself*) took a trip. The teacher blamed Joe and *me* (not *myself*).

NEGRO. Always capitalize. See *BLACK.*

NOR. See *OR.*

NUMBER. See *AMOUNT.*

OFF OF. The *of* is unnecessary. She jumped off (of) the bridge.

O.K., OKAY, OKE. Do not use in formal writing.

ONE OF THE MOST. Verbiage. Eliminate *one of.* (One of) the most beautiful girl (s) I know . . .

OR, NOR. Use *or* with *either; nor* with *neither.* Wrong: *Neither* the coach *or* his team . . . Right: *Neither* the coach *nor* his team . . .

OUTSIDE OF. The *of* is unnecessary. Outside (of) the school. *Outside of* is informal for *except, besides.* Do not use. Wrong: *Outside of* a few boys, nobody was home. Right: *Except for* a few boys, nobody was home.

OVER WITH. Do not use informally for *finished, completed.*

PLUS. Do not use for *and.* Wrong: He needed paper, erasers, *plus* pencils.

QUITE, RATHER. Avoid these qualifiers: She was (quite) sick and (rather) unhappy.

J 14

Choice of Word

RAISE, RISE. Know the principal parts and meanings of these verbs.
>   Raise (to lift up); raised; (have) raised; (is) raising.
>   Rise (to move upward);   rose; (have) risen; (is) rising.
>   *Raise* is a transitive verb and generally takes an object. Examples: he *raises* the window, he has *raised* the window. *Rise* is an intransitive verb and generally is followed by an adverb phrase. Examples: I *rise* in the morning; I have *risen* in the morning.

RATHER. See *QUITE.*

RIGHT AWAY. Overused. Do not use informally for *immediately, continuously, at once.*

SET, SIT. Know the principal parts and meanings of these verbs.
>   Set (to put) set; (have) set; (is) setting.
>   Sit (to rest) sat; (have) sat; (is) sitting.
>   *Set* is a transitive verb and generally takes an object. Examples: He *set* the book on the table; he *had set* the book on the table. *Sit* is an intransitive verb and generally is followed by an adverb phrase. Examples: He *sits* in the chair; he *had sat* in the chair.

SHAPE. Do not use informally for *condition.* Use *shape* for *figure, pattern, character.*

Choice of Word

SNUCK. The principal parts are regular: *sneak, sneaking, sneaked.* Not *sneak, sneaking, snack, SNUCK.*

SURE. Do not use informally for *certainly, surely, indeed.*

TELL, TOLD. Primarily used to introduce indirect statements, NOT direct. Weak: Mother *told* me, "Don't do that." (Use *order, instruct.*)

THE. For misuse of, see *A, AN, THE.*

THING. Do not use for *duty, fashion, compulsion.* Wrong: She has a *thing* about baldheaded men. The macroshirt is the latest *thing.* Let the teachers do their *thing.*

TRY AND. Do not use *and* for *to* with the infinitive. Wrong: Try *and* be here. Right: Try *to* be here.

UNIQUE. Means *only one of its kind.* It cannot be qualified. It is impossible to be (quite) unique, (very) unique, (almost) unique.

USE TO. The past tense is always *used to* with the *-d.*

VERY. 'Constantly overused. *Very* should be followed by *much* or *greatly* when it modifies a verb or participle. Right: She was *very much* delighted.

J**14**

Choice of Word

WHERE.   Cannot take the place of *that*. Wrong: I heard *where* he was fired for impertinence. Right: I heard *that* he was fired for impertinence.

WHITE.   Never capitalize *white* referring to race.

-WISE.   Avoid as a suffix (see also 14G.) Appallingly overused in strained, awkward neologisms. Wrong: *ideawise, housewifewise, newswise.* Easily avoided by using the expression *by way of.* For example: *By way of* ideas . . . However, standard words such as *likewise, lengthwise, clockwise,* and *otherwise* are acceptable. When in doubt, use a dictionary.

Choice of Word

**REVIEW
EXERCISE**

DIRECTIONS: Rewrite each paragraph to correct the italicized words.

Part I

Yesterday a *couple* of *guys* and *myself* had a *fun* time and *snuck* into a deserted house. There were a large *amount* of crates on the floor, and we *figured* that the owner had *made up* his mind to move. We *guessed* the owner *use to* be *aggravated* by the traffic and decided to move *further* into the country.

Part II

Most always, my father is calm, but once he *got mad* at me. *Being as* I am even-tempered, I thought my father was *mean. Firstly,* he *claimed* I had taken some cookies, and *secondly* he *inferred* I was lying. After my father was *done* speaking, I went to my room. It was *rather* dark there, but after a while, I began to feel *O.K.*

Part III

One of the most pitiful stories I have heard was about *a indian* who *immigrated* from the United States. In a *strange-looking* country, he had the *allusion* that he was different *than* other people. *Due to* his poverty, he was in *bad shape.* Eventually he *hung* himself.

Part IV

In the newspaper, Enoch read *where* a *kid* he knew had *lept off of* the roof while playing Superman. *All of a sudden,* a neighbor who was *setting* on his lawn noticed the *kid. Hero-wise,* the neighbor saved the lad *right away.* When Enoch was *over with* reading the article, he left the house to *meet up with* his wife.

Wordiness and Repetition

15 A AVOID WORDINESS AND NEEDLESS REPETITION.

Avoid carelessly used words or phrases that repeat themselves or that are essentially synonymous.

WRONG:	The young people decided to take the *cars*. When they had all the *cars* full, they headed for the movie theater. (Needless repetition of *cars*.)
BETTER:	Having decided to take the cars, the young people crowded into them and headed for the movie theater.
WRONG:	These *happenings happened* many times.
BETTER:	These events occurred many times.
CARELESS:	The *the* book was lost. On the way back we heard *a* gunfire.

15 B DO NOT WRITE THE SAME IDEA TWICE IN DIFFERENT WORDS.

WRONG:	We always enjoy Caroline's parties. It is fun to be at them.

15 A
B

Wordiness and Repetition

WORDY EXPRESSIONS

C **ELIMINATE WORDS OR PHASES THAT CLUTTER THE
SENTENCE.**

Avoid in particular such space fillers as *I think, in my opinion,
it seems to me, as I have shown.*

The words in parentheses below clutter the sentences and take away from
their effectiveness.

(In my opinion) Woodrow Wilson was a great President.

(The reason that) we like the Mets (is) because they have a colorful
manager.

Damon (is a man who) enjoys fishing, and (I think) he likes to go
to Montana.

The boys met (up with) the girls.

Other expressions that clutter	*Alternatives*
all but ready	nearly ready
all too often	often
as a usual rule	usually
due to the fact that	because
owing to the fact	because
the fact that he did not come	his failure to arrive
There was a church on Main St.	The church on Main St.
There was this man who had an ugly dog.	A man had an ugly dog.

185

Wordiness and Repetition

CLUTTER

15 D **REDUCE WORDS OR PHRASES THAT CLUTTER SENTENCES BY CHANGING CLAUSES TO PHRASES, OR BY CHANGING PHRASES TO SINGLE WORDS.**

EXAMPLES OF CLAUSES CHANGED TO PHRASES:

Clause: *After the boys had arrived at the school,* they decided that their time was wasted.

Phrase: *Having arrived at the school* (participle phrase), the boys decided that their time was wasted.

Clause: *When August arrives,* the natives on Cape Cod always complain about the tourists.

Phrase: *During August* (prepositional phrase), the natives on Cape Cod always complain about the tourists.

Clause: Peggy, *who is a class leader,* was reelected.

Phrase: Peggy, *a class leader* (appositional phrase), was reelected.

EXAMPLES OF PHRASES CHANGED TO SINGLE WORDS:

Phrase: *All of a sudden,* the lightning struck the tree.

Single Word: *Suddenly* the lightning struck the tree.

Phrase: *That man from Wales* is a magnificent actor.

Single Word: *That Welshman* is a magnificent actor.

15 D

Wordiness and Repetition

REDUNDANCY

E DO NOT USE WORDS OR PHRASES THAT ARE REDUNDANT.

COMMENT: Redundancy here applies to those words within a phrase
that repeat the idea already expressed.

EXAMPLE: Now at this time (*Now* and *at this time* mean exactly
the same thing; one or the other is redundant and can be
eliminated.)

Redundant Expressions	*Alternatives*
ascend up	ascend
circulate around	circulate
consensus of opinion	consensus
continue on	continue
escape out	escape
final result	result
hopeful optimism	**optimism**
important essentials	essentials
large in size	large, sizable
many in number	many
meet together	meet
meet up with	meet
new creation	creation
perfectly correct	correct
red in color	red
refer back	refer
repeat again	repeat
ten in number	ten
true facts	facts
unexpected surprise	surprise
wealthy millionaire	millionaire
widow of the late President	**widow of the President**

E 15

Wordiness and Repetition

FLOWERY STYLE

15 **F** **REWRITE SENTENCES THAT HAVE A FLOWERY, SELF-CONSCIOUS STYLE. WRITE NATURALLY.**
(See also 13Z and 14I.)

Example of a flowery, self-conscious style:

> A thick mizzle lay delicately in little puffs over the fen and pungent air; the snakes were hunting, slimy and sinister. Water snakes hissed a monody as they searched through the swamp.

Less pretentious:

> A damp mist covered the swamp, its air thick, yet delicate, giving off a sour-sweet smell. Hissing in low, monotonous undertones, the slimy, sinister water moccasins searched for prey.

Even clearer:

> A damp, thick mist blanketed the fetid swamp. Hissing as they searched for food, two water moccasins slithered across the ground.

Wordiness and Repetition

REVIEW
EXERCISE

DIRECTIONS: Rewrite the sentences below to eliminate wordiness and
repetition.

1. It was on Independence Day, July 4, 1982, that Mr. Pox
   departed at 6 a.m. in the morning and left to meet up with his
   cousin.

2. All too often, the new styles today seem to be yellow in color.

3. After the secretary had arrived for dictation, Mr. Glotz dic-
   tated three letters to his secretary.

4. Because of the fact that the day was hot, Annie turned on the
   fan to circulate the air around.

5. At about 8 p.m. on Thursday night, he saw the great, huge
   moon, which was crescent in shape.

6. To decide about important essentials, I am of the opinion that
   one must first have all the true facts.

7. Miss Pintz quietly and silently tiptoed to the landing and
   then descended down the stairs.

8. Martha repeatedly whispered, "I love him," over and over
   again.

9. "You are perfectly correct that your arrival is an unexpected
   surprise," said King John, the monarch, all of a sudden.

10. Without exception, Mr. Karp always wrote his letters in ink,
    and his handwriting was small and tiny, but tidy and neat.

Omission of Important Words

NOUN   ADJ.   VERB

16 A DO NOT CARELESSLY OMIT WORDS OR PHRASES THAT HELP CLARIFY THE SENTENCE.

EXAMPLES OF NOUNS AND ADJECTIVES OMITTED:

WRONG: The minister read over the deceased.

RIGHT: The minister read a *burial service* over the deceased *man*.

WRONG: If the sea was not, the Eskimos would have perished long ago.

RIGHT: If the sea was not a *good provider*, the Eskimos would have perished long ago.

WRONG: Zeus did not do all that for the Greeks.

RIGHT: Zeus did not do all that *much good* for the Greeks.

EXAMPLES OF VERBS OMITTED:

WRONG: In an hour, I had a path to the driveway.

RIGHT: In an hour, I had *shoveled* a path to the driveway.

WRONG: My mother was leaning over me saying that I had a bad dream.

RIGHT: My mother was leaning over me saying that I had *had* a bad dream.

16 A

Omission of Important Words

PREP.   PRON.   CONJ.   ART.

B **DO NOT OMIT NECESSARY PREPOSITIONS, PRONOUNS, CONJUNCTIONS, OR ARTICLES.**

Prepositions and pronouns

UNCLEAR: The director wanted to see me once.

BETTER: The director wanted to see me *at* once.

UNCLEAR: My friend and girl stood on the sidelines.

BETTER: My friend and *his* girl stood on the sidelines.

Conjunctions and prepositions (See also 21B.)

UNCLEAR: He understood all the girls were preparing to travel by boat, train, or plane.

BETTER: He understood *that* all the girls were preparing to travel *by* boat, *by* train, or *by* plane.

NOTE: As a rule, it is wise to use *that* when introducing an *indirect statement,* particularly following verbs of feeling, saying, believing, and thinking.

B 16

Omission of Important Words

COMPARISONS

16 c DO NOT OMIT WORDS NEEDED TO COMPLETE A COMPARISON.

WRONG: Cos Cobs are milder.

RIGHT: Cos Cobs are milder *than other cigars.*

WRONG: She is the stupidest girl!

RIGHT: She is the stupidest girl *whom I have ever met.*

WRONG: She is so beautiful! (Exclamatory *so,* see 13S.)

RIGHT: She is so beautiful that the boys all admire her.

WRONG: I like bowling better than Joan.

RIGHT: I like bowling better than Joan *does.*

WRONG: This is such a dull book.

RIGHT: This is such a dull book *that everyone avoids it.*

16 c

Omission of Important Words

DIRECTIONS: Rewrite the sentences below and supply words that have been omitted.

1. Mac likes candy better than Minnie.

2. "This sundae is so good," Joan squealed.

3. Hal went on to say whatever was good for business was good for country.

4. Mrs. Eclaire is as brilliant as any woman.

5. The profession of teaching demands more time and effort.

6. The hour of our departure, my mother and I felt so excited.

7. Mr. Quince complained he was too tired.

8. Jim gave me more trouble than Sally.

9. Maine farmers say they grow larger potatoes than Idaho.

10. French wine is not always the most expensive.

11. When Ben visited the restaurant, he complained there was not enough and that he wanted more.

12. After working on beach for an hour, Alex had a beautiful sand castle.

13. I could see the hose squirting all over.

Unity of Sentences

REWRITE SENTENCES THAT DO NOT MAKE SENSE.

Do not join unrelated ideas illogically in the sentence.

UNCLEAR: He was stranded because he was in Acapulco, Mexico.

IMPROVED: He was in Acapulco, Mexico, and he was stranded.
(Unity achieved by making both ideas equal)

BETTER: When he was in Acapulco, Mexico, he found himself
stranded. (Unity achieved by subordination)

UNCLEAR: We arrived in the rainy season, but we had only two
short showers. (A gap in thought)

IMPROVED: We arrived in the rainy season, but rain fell only twice
during our stay. (Unity achieved by making both ideas
equal and repeating word for emphasis)

BETTER: Although we arrived in the rainy season, rain fell only
twice during our stay. (Unity achieved by subordination)

Unity of Sentences

B   REWRITE SENTENCES TO EXCLUDE EXCESSIVE DETAIL.

WORDY: He lives in Truro, a small town on Cape Cod, which in winter has only six hundred inhabitants, but in the summer has close to five thousand in it, with his parents whom he helps support in their old age.

NOTE: Writers should make up their minds which of the two ideas is more important and stick to that idea.

DIRECT: He lives in Truro, Cape Cod, which in winter only has six hundred inhabitants, but which in the summer has a population of close to five thousand.

WORDY: He decided to assassinate the dictator with a bow and arrow that he had bought at a bargain sale in Macy's basement. (Which is the essential detail: the bow and arrow, or the bargain sale?)

B 17

Unity of Sentences

17 C   DO NOT USE THE DOUBLE NEGATIVE.

COMMENT: There are many informal expressions where two negatives are used in the same sentence. Avoid them in formal writing.

Popular double negatives	*Alternatives*
can't hardly	can hardly
can't scarcely	can scarcely
can't help but admire	can't help admiring
not hardly enough	hardly enough
couldn't find nowhere	couldn't find anywhere
wasn't but one	was but one

17 c

Unity of Sentences

D   SUPPORT GENERALIZATIONS WITH OBJECTIVE FACTS OR EXAMPLES.

WRONG: Everyone in the class liked *Johnny Tremain*. It was fast-moving, interesting, and would make a fine movie.

RIGHT: Everyone in the class liked *Johnny Tremain*. When we took a vote, we all agreed that it would make a fine movie.

7 E   QUALIFY GENERALIZATIONS ACCURATELY, AND SUPPORT THEM WITH FACTS OR EXAMPLES.

Qualifying adjectives	*Qualifying adverbs*
All	Without exception, always
Most	Often, mostly, chiefly
Many	Generally, commonly
Some	Sometimes
Few	Almost never, seldom
No, none	Never

WRONG: *All* American children are spoiled. (This overstated generalization calls for precise judgment supported by fact or example.)

RIGHT: *Most* (or *many*) American children are spoiled. According to a recent edition of *Time* magazine, American parents spent an average of $100 per child on toys last year.

D
E **17**

Coordination and Subordination

COORDINATING CONJUNCTIONS

18 WRITE SENTENCES THAT CORRECTLY COORDINATE AND SUBORDINATE THE MAIN IDEAS.

18 A USE THE CORRECT COORDINATING CONJUNCTION TO JOIN IDEAS OF *EQUAL* IMPORTANCE.

Coordinating Conjunctions

And is used to add one idea to another.
But is used to contrast one idea to another.
For is used to mean *because*.
Nor (neither, nor) } are used to express *choice* between one
Or (either, or) } idea and another.

ADDITION: I will sell the jewels, *and* she will give you the money.

CONTRAST: I will sell the jewels, *but* she will give you the money.

CHOICE: *Either* I will sell the jewels, *or* she will give you the money.

WRONG: I will go to school, *and* I will not like it.

RIGHT: I will go to school, *but* I will not like it.

UNCLEAR: We received invitations, *but* so did the Smiths.

BETTER: We received invitations, *and* so did the Smiths.

UNCLEAR: Bruce ate the banana, *and* he was hungry.

BETTER: Bruce ate the banana, *for* he was hungry.

18 A

Coordination and Subordination

SUBORDINATING CONJUNCTIONS

8 B   **USE THE CORRECT SUBORDINATING CONJUNCTION TO JOIN IDEAS OF *UNEQUAL* IMPORTANCE.**

Subordinating Conjunctions Expressing Time:

as		
after	since	when
before	until	while

Subordinating Conjunctions Expressing Cause:

because	in as much as	since

NOTE: Avoid using *as* as a causal conjunction in place of *because.* Use it as a temporal conjunction. (Example: she called the doctor *because* [not *as*] she was sick.) *Since* is becoming primarily a temporal conjunction.

Subordinating Conjunctions Expressing Purpose, Result:

that	in order that	so that

Subordinating Conjunctions Expressing Condition:

although	unless	if

FAULTY: *Because* he had graduated from medical school, he decided to join the Army.

BETTER: *After* he had graduated from medical school, he decided to join the Army.

(Continued on next page.)

B 18

Coordination and Subordination

SUBORDINATING CONJUNCTIONS

FAULTY: *Although* Pat wants to go with us, she must be on time.

BETTER: *If* Pat wants to go with us, she must be on time.

BETTER: *Although* Pat wants to go with us, she has not showed up yet.

NOTE: *Although* primarily means *despite the fact that.*

Coordination and Subordination

18 C REWRITE SENTENCES THAT ARE INCORRECTLY COORDINATED. PLACE THE LESSER IDEA IN A SUBORDINATE CLAUSE.

WEAK: The sun was shining, *and* the rain was falling.

STRONGER: *Although it was raining,* the sun was shining.

WEAK: Per Hansa finally reached Spring Creek, *and* soon other pioneers began to arrive.

STRONGER: *After Per Hansa had reached Spring Creek,* other settlers began to arrive.

WEAK: The assembly hall was crowded, *and* there was a good deal of noise.

STRONGER: *Because the assembly hall was crowded,* it was very noisy.

c**18**

Coordination and Subordination

INCORRECT SUBORDINATION

18 D REWRITE SENTENCES THAT INCORRECTLY SUBORDINATE THE PRINCIPAL IDEA. PLACE THE LESSER IDEA IN A SUBORDINATE CLAUSE.

WEAK: One day Jody was hoeing the garden *when he saw Flag eating the corn.*

STRONGER: One day, *as Jody was hoeing the garden,* he saw Flag eating the corn.

WEAK: Thomas Cipher was cleaning his gun one day *when he decided to commit suicide.*

STRONG: One day, *when Thomas Cipher was cleaning his gun,* he decided to commit suicide.

WEAK: The children were becoming tired and irritable *when they decided to call home for help.*

STRONG: *When the children became tired and irritable,* they decided to call home for help.

Coordination and Subordination

**REVIEW
EXERCISE**

DIRECTIONS: **Part I.** Rewrite the sentences below so that they are correctly subordinated. (Note: Do *not* coordinate.)

1. When I lost my way, I was going home.

2. George accidentally killed the rabbit, and he was cutting the grass.

3. Caspar was a teacher, and so he had a long summer vacation.

4. I lent him the car, but he asked for it.

5. They stopped at the motel, and they had been driving all day and were tired.

6. I saw the red light, and it was too late to stop.

7. My mother studied with an expert since she is a good cook.

8. Josie thought she was going mad, and she visited a psychiatrist.

9. When she tapped her feet rhythmically, the band was playing.

10. As I had seen the opera, I decided to buy the record.

DIRECTIONS: **Part II.** Revise the following passage to achieve proper subordination.

I was reading *Ivanhoe* when I thought I heard a noise. It was late at night. I put the book down and went downstairs to investigate. I looked in the dining room. I looked in the living room. I found nothing suspicious. I decided to return to my bedroom when I heard the noise again. It seemed to be coming from the garage. I had only thought that I heard the noise the first time. Now I was quite certain of the sound. I dashed to the garage, and I saw a raccoon trapped under a crate. I lifted the crate and freed the raccoon. Then I walked back to the house and went to bed.

Reference of Pronouns

19   EVERY PRONOUN MUST REFER CLEARLY TO ITS PARTICULAR ANTECEDENT.

> NOTE: The pronoun must always agree with its antecedent in gender, number, and person. (See also 11L-11O.)

19 A   DO NOT START A PARAGRAPH OR COMPOSITION WITH A PRONOUN THAT HAS NO ANTECEDENT, OR WITH A PRONOUN THAT REFERS TO THE TITLE.
(See also 13R and 13U.)

WRONG: A Long Hike

When *we* were hiking one beautiful summer's day, a car drew up beside *us*.

RIGHT: When *my father and I* were hiking one beautiful summer's day, a car drew up beside us.

WRONG: School Days

This is *something* I have always wanted to write about.

RIGHT: Whitehall School has provided me with many exciting and humorous experiences.

WRONG: *Great Expectations*
This is a book about love and maturity.

RIGHT: Dickens' novel *Great Expectations* is about love and maturity.

19 **A**

Reference of Pronouns

9 B REWRITE THE SENTENCE TO MAKE CLEAR WHICH ANTECEDENT IS MEANT WHEN A PRONOUN HAS TWO POSSIBLE ALTERNATIVES.

Techniques for improving clarity:
> 1) Use a synonym for the antecedent.
> 2) Repeat the antecedent.
> 3) Change the construction of the sentence.
> 4) Quote the exact words of the speaker.

VAGUE: The teacher told Wendy that *she* would be on time tomorrow.

BETTER
BUT
AWKWARD: The teacher told Wendy that she expected *Wendy* to be on time tomorrow. (Repetition of antecedent)

BETTER: The teacher told Wendy that she expected *her* to be on time tomorrow. (Change of construction and use of a pronoun)

> or

The teacher told Wendy that she *intended to be* on time tomorrow.

BETTER: The teacher said, "Wendy, I will be on time tomorrow."

> or

The teacher said, "Wendy, I expect you to be on time tomorrow."

B 19

Reference of Pronouns

VAGUE *THIS, THAT, WHICH*

19 C   REWRITE THE SENTENCE THAT VAGUELY USES *THIS, THAT, WHICH* TO REFER TO AN IDEA IMPLIED IN THE PRECEDING SENTENCE OR PARAGRAPH.
(See also 13U.)

COMMENT: One of the most frequent errors found in compositions is the use of pronouns referring *vaguely* to an action or event that precedes the subordinate clause. Correct usage *demands* that the action or event be specified by the use of repetition, by apposition, or by rephrasing the sentence.

THE PRONOUN IN THE ENGLISH LANGUAGE MUST ALWAYS REFER TO A SPECIFIC, NAMED ANTECEDENT.

VAGUE: I decided to give up smoking, *which* pleased my wife.

RIGHT: I decided to give up smoking, a decision which pleased my wife.

VAGUE: The union decided to support the new President. *This* certainly pleased the conservatives.

RIGHT: *That the union decided to support the new President* certainly pleased the conservatives.

RIGHT: The union decided to support the new President, *an action* (*a decision, a maneuver*) that certainly pleased the conservatives.

RIGHT: *The union's decision to support the new President* certainly pleased the conservatives.

19 c

Reference of Pronouns

IMPERSONAL PRONOUNS

9 D **REWRITE THE SENTENCE THAT USES THE VAGUE, INDEFINITE *IT, YOU, WE, THEY*.**
(See also 13U.)

COMMENT: The student is advised to ask whether or not he is really addressing the teacher when he writes: "*You* should always take a shower before breakfast."

WRONG: In this book *it* says that puppy love seldom develops into a mature relationship.

BETTER: *The book states* that puppy love seldom develops into a mature relationship.

EVEN *The Art of Loving* states that puppy love seldom devel-
BETTER: ops into a mature relationship.

WRONG: At school *they* say that *you* should not answer back. *You* just do what *you* are told and smile happily.

BETTER: At school our *dean* says that *students* should not answer back. *They* do what *they* are told and smile happily.

D 19

Reference of Pronouns

DIRECTIONS: Rewrite the following sentences to correct vague reference of the italicized pronouns.

1. The President appointed Billings to the Supreme Court, and *this* pleased *him* very much.

2. Percy told Harry that *he* had bad breath but that *this* could be remedied by breath mints.

3. *They* say that a new bridge will be built over Long Island Sound, *which they* say is too bad.

4. Since my mother is a doctor, it is possible that I may do *that*.

5. When the storm broke, *we* ran out of *it* and into the safety of the house.

6. Pearl said that Martha was sick and that *she* was having marital problems, but *she* did not want to talk about *it, which* is just as well.

7. In the Army, *you* do what *you* are told, and *you* are not supposed to have any ideas of *your* own.

8. Paul wanted to become a writer, *which* irritated his wife.

9. The United States has a two-party system, but *they* say that *this* is not true of many other countries.

10. Martha told Phyllis that *she* had made a mistake but that *it* could be easily corrected.

Use of Modifiers

WORDS

A PLACE WORDS AS CLOSELY AS POSSIBLE TO THE WORDS THEY MODIFY.

COMMENT: Place the adverbs *not, almost, even, ever, nearly, only* immediately before the words they modify.

Consider the various possibilities of *only:*

My teacher said he *only* wanted to fail me.

My teacher *only* said he wanted to fail me.

My teacher said he wanted to fail *only* me.

My teacher said *only* he wanted to fail me.

My *only* teacher said he wanted to fail me.

Only my teacher said he wanted to fail me.

A 20

Use of Modifiers

PHRASES

20 B **PLACE PHRASES AND CLAUSES CLOSE TO THE WORDS THEY MODIFY.**

PHRASE MISPLACED: The headmaster talked to us about school spirit *during assembly.*

CLEAR: *During assembly* the headmaster talked to us about school spirit.

CLAUSE MISPLACED: *When I was in graduate school,* I remember all the interesting discussions we had.

CLEAR: I remember all the interesting discussions we had *when I was in graduate school.*

20 C **AVOID SQUINTING MODIFIERS — CONSTRUCTIONS THAT MAY REFER EITHER TO THE PRECEDING OR TO THE FOLLOWING WORD.**

SQUINTING: The teachers were encouraged *immediately* to give her a second chance.

CLEAR: The teachers *immediately* were encouraged to give her a second chance.

CLEAR: The teachers were encouraged to give her a second chance *immediately.*

20 **B**
C

Use of Modifiers

O D DO NOT AWKWARDLY SPLIT AN INFINITIVE.

COMMENT: An *infinitive* is generally made up of *to* followed by a verb, and may be used as a noun, an adjective, or an adverb. (See Appendix 3, p. 241.)

SPLIT INFINITIVE: Do not try to, *for the sheer pleasure of it,* split the infinitive.

IMPROVED: Do not try to split the infinitive, for the sheer pleasure of it.

SPLIT INFINITIVE: He tried to *rapidly and accurately* finish the examination.

IMPROVED: He tried to finish the examination *rapidly and accurately*.

D 20

Use of Modifiers

DANGLING MODIFIERS

20 E   AVOID DANGLING VERBAL PHRASES AND ELLIPTICAL CLAUSES.

COMMENT: *A dangling verbal phrase* modifies a word in such a way that the final sentence becomes absurd.

1) *Dangling participle*

WRONG: Walking on the beach, the stars seemed brighter than ever. (Did the stars walk?)

RIGHT: Walking on the beach, we noticed that the stars seemed brighter than ever.

2) *Dangling gerund*

WRONG: After examining the wet grounds, the game was called off. (Did the game examine the wet grounds?)

RIGHT: After the umpires had examined the wet grounds, they called off the game.

3) *Dangling infinitive*

WRONG: To do well on the examination, careful instruction must be received. (Is the instruction trying to do well?)

RIGHT: To do well on the examination, we must receive careful instruction.

(Continued on next page.)

20 E

Use of Modifiers

4)   *Dangling elliptical clause*

WRONG: When steamed until tender, remove the corn from the pot. (*Corn* is understood in the elliptical clause.)

RIGHT: When the corn is steamed until it is tender, remove it from the pot.

E 20

Use of Modifiers

DANGLING MODIFIERS

20 F AN ABSOLUTE PHRASE CONSISTS OF A NOUN MODIFIED BY A PARTICIPLE PHRASE BUT THAT IS GRAMMATICALLY INDEPENDENT OF THE REST OF THE SENTENCE.

COMMENT: An absolute phrase is a group of words (similar to the Latin ablative absolute) that has no grammatical relationship to the words in the main clause.

NOTE: An absolute is permitted in English but is risky. It does not dangle, however, because the word to which the participle refers is within the phrase itself.

Absolute phrases:

Our homework having been satisfactorily completed, we were allowed to watch television.

The class having assembled quietly, Dr. Learned proceeded to give it a tongue lashing.

20 F

Use of Modifiers

DIRECTIONS: Rewrite the sentences below to correct misused modifiers.

1. The sign on the soft drink machine read, "Only deposit quarters."

2. Speakers who lecture too often are forgotten.

3. While waiting for the bus, my paper fell into a puddle.

4. When six years old, Alfred's uncle took him to the zoo.

5. In planning a new building, careful drawings must first be made.

6. When an undergraduate at Yale, a baseball hit my father in the head.

7. Irma wanted him to always and passionately love her.

8. Ben promised even to love her until he died.

9. While shaving in the bathroom, the phone rang.

10. People who exercise frequently are sensible.

11. At the dinner table, West Point plebes are not permitted to talk.

12. Entering the room, broken chairs and tables were seen.

13. Carrie is as tall as her sister almost.

14. The stricken vessel began to slowly and gradually sink beneath the waves.

15. When I was a baby, I remember the attention given me by my uncle and aunt.

Parallelism

PLACE SIMILAR IDEAS OR ELEMENTS IN A SENTENCE IN PARALLEL GRAMATICAL FORM.

COMMENT: The correct use of parallelism conveys to the reader with impact the force of equal ideas. It is the mark of an emphatic, vigorous style. The simplest form of parallelism involves two or more words in a series, but the skilled writer will use the more complex parallelism of phrases, verbals, subordinate clauses, independent clauses or even sentences.

A Chart to Demonstrate Parallelism

Nouns
She has *poise, beauty,* and *arrogance.*

Adjectives
She is *charming, gracious,* and *stupid.*

Verbs
She *hissed, booed,* and *cat-called.*

Participles
Telling lies and spreading gossip, she lost her friends.

Gerunds
She lost her friends *by telling lies* and *by spreading gossip.*

Infinitives
She liked *to tell lies* and *to spread gossip.*

Phrases
She is a girl *of poise, of beauty,* and *of arrogance.*

Clauses
She said *that she liked to dance* and *that she found boys useful.* (Noun clauses here are parallel.)

Parallelism

A REWRITE SENTENCES THAT LACK PARALLELISM BASED ON FAULTY COORDINATION OF:
      1) REGULAR PARTS OF SPEECH
      2) PHRASES
      3) VERBALS
      4) VOICE (ACTIVE AND PASSIVE)
      5) CLAUSES (INDEPENDENT AND SUBORDINATE)

(See chart, p. 216.)

Nouns, adjectives, and verbs

WRONG: She was fat with a bad temper. (*Fat* is an adjective; *with a bad temper* is a phrase.)

RIGHT: She was *fat* and *bad-tempered.* (Adjectives)

RIGHT: She *weighed two hundred pounds* and *had a bad temper.* (Verbs and nouns)

Verbals

WRONG: Destroying art is vandalism, but to kill animals is sport. (*Destroying* is a gerund; *to kill* an infinitive.)

RIGHT: *Destroying* art is vandalism, but *killing* animals is sport. (Gerunds)

(Continued on next page.)

A 21

Parallelism

FAULTY PARALLELISM

Voice

WRONG: He sailed to Africa, and many animals have been shot by
          him. (*Sailed* is active; *have been shot* passive.)

RIGHT: He *sailed* to Africa and *shot* many animals. (Both verbs
          active)

Clauses

WRONG: The coach talked of good conditioning and that Yale
          had a strong team. (Independent clause parallel with
          subordinate clause)

RIGHT: *The coach talked of good conditioning,* and *he said that
          Yale had a strong team.* (Parallel independent clauses)

RIGHT: The coach talked *of good conditioning* and *of Yale's
          strong team.* (Parallel phrases)

RIGHT: The coach declared *that good conditioning was
          important* and *that Yale had a strong team.* (Parallel
          subordinate clauses)

21 B

Parallelism

B **REWRITE SENTENCES THAT LACK PARALLELISM BASED ON CARELESS OMISSION OF:**
        1) ARTICLES
        2) CONJUNCTIONS
        3) PREPOSITIONS
        4) VERBS

WEAK: Mima's pocketbook contained a lipstick and compact. (Article omitted)

STRONGER: Mima's pocketbook contained *a* lipstick and *a* compact.

WEAK: Jimmy had difficulty in learning the subject and studying his lessons. (Preposition omitted)

STRONGER: Jimmy had difficulty *in* learning the subject and *in* studying his lessons.

WEAK: I know that you are young and you are ambitious. (Subordinating conjunction omitted)

STRONGER: I know *that* you are young and *that* you are ambitious.

WEAK: Poppy had visited the zoo and seen many animals. (Auxiliary verb *had* omitted.)

STRONGER: Poppy *had* visited the zoo and *had* seen many animals.

B 21

Parallelism

DIRECTIONS: Rewrite the sentences below to revise faulty parallelism.

1. Horace learned how to load a rifle and the technique of shooting.

2. Amanda had hoped for a high Latin grade but failed her final examination.

3. Find time to do your homework and sweep the kitchen.

4. What Ahab needed was a quiet night's rest and nourishing meal.

5. Quincy was charming, brilliant, and had a lot of money.

6. General Hox was despised by his aides, his soldiers, and the townspeople hated him, too.

7. Walking is fine exercise, but to ride is the sport of kings.

8. Examine the crab and how it can walk sideways.

9. The play was witty, delightful, and a financial success.

10. T.J. spoke with articulation, with authority, and stylishly.

11. Grace was ambitious with a burning desire to be the first woman President.

12. Hank had been to Paris four times and visited the bistros on the Left Bank.

13. Heather enjoyed art, and many fine paintings were completed by her.

14. Griselda was nasty, unprincipled, and had curiosity.

15. Kay enjoyed hiking and reading, and tennis was a sport she liked, too.

Variety of Style

2   VARY THE TYPE AND LENGTH OF SENTENCES TO AVOID THE HUMDRUM, MONOTONOUS STYLE.

2 A   DO NOT WRITE A SERIES OF SENTENCES FOLLOWING A SUBJECT-VERB PATTERN.

HUMDRUM: My *father is* a good man. *He goes* to work faithfully every day. *He brings* home a paycheck every Friday. He *gives* it to Mother. *She puts* it in the bank regularly every Monday morning.

BETTER: My father, a good man, goes to work faithfully every day. On Fridays he brings home a paycheck, which he gives to Mother. Regularly, every Monday morning, she puts it in the bank.

Devices used to break subject-verb monotony:

Simple modifiers
     Faithfully, my father goes to work.

Appositional elements
     A good man, my father . . .

Participle phrases
     Having finished his work, my father . . .

Prepositional phrases
     On Fridays my father brings home . . .

Clauses
     When my father comes home on Fridays, he . . .

A 22

Variety of Style

SHORT, CHOPPY SENTENCES

22 B DO NOT WRITE A SERIES OF SHORT, CHOPPY SENTENCES.

NOTE: Rules 22A and 22B generally overlap, but 22B is even more the mark of a childish style.

CHOPPY: I like gum drops. They are delicious. They are very inexpensive. I buy them on Fridays. My mother takes me to the store. It is a candy store. It is on Greenwich Avenue.

BETTER: I like gum drops because they are delicious and inexpensive. On Fridays my mother takes me to the candy store on Greenwich Avenue.

Devices used to avoid short, choppy sentences:

1) Use the methods suggested in 22A.

2) Combine simple sentences into compound or complex sentences.

CHOPPY: My mother is kind. I like her.

IMPROVED: I like my mother because she is kind.

3) Change the pattern of the sentence.

CHOPPY: I like sourballs. They are easy on my throat.

IMPROVED: Easy on my throat, sourballs have always been my favorite candy.

22 B

222

Variety of Style

22 C **DO NOT WRITE LONG, LOOSE. STRINGY SENTENCES USING *AND, AND ALSO, AND SO, AND THEN, BUT.***
(See also 13O.)

NEVER-ENDING SENTENCE:	My Dad and I decided to go fishing *and* it was a Saturday *and* we headed for the river *and then* decided to cast our lines.
MUCH IMPROVED:	Because it was a Saturday, Dad and I decided to go fishing. After we had reached the river, we decided to cast our lines.
STRINGY:	Chip may arrive tomorrow, *but* I will warn him not to come, *but* do not forget to remind me to call him.
IMPROVED:	Chip may arrive tomorrow, but I will warn him not to come. Please do not forget to remind me to call him.

C **22**

Variety of Style

22 D USE A VARIETY OF TRANSITIONAL WORDS TO KEEP SENTENCES FLOWING SMOOTHLY AND SWIFTLY.

Transitional words and expressions: (See also 23E.)

Addition: moreover, further, furthermore, besides, also, too, again, in addition, next, first, finally, at last. (Be careful of *and, and so, and then, and also.)*

Contrast: but, yet, however, still, nevertheless, after all, at the same time, on the other hand.

Comparison: similarly, in the same way, as if.

Purpose: for this reason, in order to, so that.

Result: therefore, as a result, so that.

Time: meanwhile, finally, at length, immediately, soon, still, after a short time, afterward, later.

Place: here, nearby, close at hand, beyond, on the other side.

Conclusion: to sum up, on the whole, indeed, in short.

Example: for example, for instance, in fact.

22 D

Variety of Style

REVIEW
EXERCISE

DIRECTIONS: Rewrite each paragraph below to achieve a smooth,
varied style. Reduce to four or five sentences.

I.   Pierre was a chef. He worked at the Algonquin Hotel. Pierre had
been trained in Paris at the Cordon Bleu. He was born in Boston. Pierre
specialized in one dish. This dish was braised prunes. Pierre told me the
recipe of this dish. First stew the prunes. Then soak them in soda
overnight. Last put them under the broiler for one minute. The result is
prunes a la Pierre. They are delicious.

II.   Elizabeth I was Queen of England. She died in the early part of the
17th century. She was very popular with her subjects. They called
her Good Queen Bess. She was composed and dignified in public. She
was willful and bad-tempered in private. Many people think that queens
are pure and regal. Elizabeth enjoyed hearing bawdy stories and gossip.

III.   I like my uncle. His name is Ronald. He lives in Louisiana.
He is the president of a bank in Shreveport. My uncle visits our family
once a year. He comes at Christmastime. He always brings a present
for me. The present is money.

IV.   Going to my dentist is no fun. My dentist cleans my teeth twice a
year. He takes X-rays of my teeth. Sometimes he finds a cavity. My
dentist first drills it. Then he fills the cavity. The drilling does not hurt.
My dentist uses a pain killer. My dentist would not try to hurt me. He
is a kind man.

Paragraphing

23 A **USE A TOPIC SENTENCE TO STATE THE MAIN IDEA OF EACH PARAGRAPH.**

NOTE: When introducing a new idea, be sure to indent and begin a new paragraph using a topic sentence.

DEFINITION OF A PARAGRAPH:

A *paragraph* explains, defends, describes, focuses on one topic by the use of closely related sentences.

DEFINITIONS OF A TOPIC SENTENCE AND A CLINCHER SENTENCE:

The *topic sentence* states or summarizes the main idea of the paragraph.

A *clincher sentence* concludes or summarizes the main idea of a paragraph.

GENERAL RULES FOR PARAGRAPHING:
1.) Start a new paragraph to begin a new idea.
2.) Start with a topic sentence, or end with a clincher.
3.) Develop the facts from your outline.
4.) Use concrete, specific details.
5.) Use transitional words between sentences. (See 22D.)
6.) CONCENTRATE ON THE MAIN IDEA OF THE PARAGRAPH.

23 **A**

Paragraphing

23 B WRITE PARAGRAPHS THAT STICK TO THE SAME TOPIC AND THAT HAVE LOGIC AND ORDER.

COMMENT: End the paragraph when the topic, situation, or setting is exhausted, or when there is a change of speaker in dialogue. (See 5H.)

OVERLOADED PARAGRAPH:

> Tennis is quickly becoming a very popular pastime in America. Of course, television is popular, too. Tennis is fast-moving and does not require much money to begin. Some people, however, like to cook for a hobby. Most of my family plays tennis.

NOTE: Not only does the paragraph above stray from the topic ("Tennis is becoming popular"), but it also lacks COHERENCE. That is, the paragraph has neither *order* nor *logic*.

PARAGRAPH TOPIC CLARIFIED:

> Tennis is quickly becoming a very popular pastime in America, according to Phil Ochs, a tennis promoter. When asked why this was so, Ochs gave three reasons. First, tennis does not require much money to begin. Second, it fits nicely into the current physical fitness mania in the United States. And finally, tennis players find they can play the sport for an entire lifetime.

Paragraphing

POOR DEVELOPMENT

23 C REWRITE PARAGRAPHS IN WHICH THE TOPIC SENTENCE IS
SUPPORTED BY TOO MANY GENERALIZATIONS.

POOR: Most people like to get their own way. That is, they
usually like things to go the way they planned them.
Planning ahead assures many people that they will get
what they want. Getting one's own way is a source of
satisfaction for many individuals.

NOTE: The paragraph above is a series of general statements leading
nowhere.

BETTER: Most people like to get their own way. My father, for
example, is very happy when he sells a car to a customer. Sometimes he shows his sense of pleasure by taking
my mother and me out to dinner. Since Mother dislikes
cooking, she has her own way, too.

Paragraphing

D DO NOT WRITE ONE-SENTENCE PARAGRAPHS EXCEPT IN DIALOGUE.

(For exceptions in dialogue, see 5H.)
No examples are required here.

TRANSITIONAL DEVICES

E USE TRANSITIONAL WORDS AND CONNECTIVES TO BRING PARAGRAPHS INTO CLOSE RELATIONSHIP WITH EACH OTHER.

Devices for transition:

1) Repeat a key word, phrase, or sentence from the preceding paragraph.
2) Use pronouns that refer to specific words in the preceding paragraph.
3) Use connectives.

Some useful connectives: (See also 22D.)

also	fortunately	of course
after that	furthermore	on the contrary
at this point	here	on the other hand
again	however	similarly
accordingly	indeed	soon
as a result	in short	still
as previously stated	meanwhile	temporarily
afterward	moreover	truly
finally	namely	thus
for example	nevertheless	while
for instance	now	

D E 23

Paragraphing : Mechanics

MECHANICS IN PARAGRAPHING

24 **FOLLOW THE CONVENTIONS FOR THE MECHANICS IN PARAGRAPHING.**

The model below illustrates the most common violations of the rules for the mechanics in paragraphing. The rules are printed on the facing page.

MODEL SHOWING VIOLATIONS
OF THE RULES FOR PARAGRAPHING

(A)   (B)

Last July my mother and fat- (C)
her gave a cookout for a-
bout ten friends. The day was hot
(D)
, and the weatherman had pre.
(D)
- dicted showers. ◄——— (E) ———►
(F)
However, my mother remarked, "
It won't rain!"

(H) ◄——————— (G) ———————►
(H) After the guests had been ser- (I)
ved their food, the rain desc- (B)
ended in torrents. Said Mother, " (F)
Goofed again!"

24   230

Paragraphing : Mechanics

24 A - 24 I

MECHANICS IN PARAGRAPHING

24 A INDENT THE FIRST WORD OF A PARAGRAPH ONE-HALF INCH. (See model on facing page.)

24 B SYLLABIFY THE LAST WORD IN A LINE CORRECTLY. (See model on facing page.)

24 C DO NOT HYPHENATE ONE- OR TWO-LETTER SYLLABLES AT THE END OF A LINE. (See model on facing page.)

24 D DO NOT BEGIN A LINE WITH A COMMA OR A HYPHEN. (See model on facing page.)

24 E DO NOT LEAVE PART OF A LINE BLANK UNLESS A NEW PARAGRAPH FOLLOWS IMMEDIATELY. (See model on facing page.)

24 F DO NOT SEPARATE QUOTATION MARKS FROM THE WORDS THEY BELONG TO. (See model on facing page.)

24 G DO NOT LEAVE A LINE BLANK BETWEEN PARAGRAPHS. (See model on facing page.)

24 H DO NOT USE ¶ AND NO ¶ SIGNS. (See model on facing page.)

24 I DO NOT HYPHENATE A ONE-SYLLABLE WORD. (See model on facing page.)

A - I **24**

Footnoting and Bibliography

MECHANICS FOR QUOTATIONS AND FOOTNOTES

25 A FOLLOW THE CONVENTIONS FOR THE MECHANICS IN QUOTING FROM A BOOK OR REFERENCE WORK.

INFORMAL ESSAYS: Keep the quotation and author's name in the text itself and avoid footnotes.

EXAMPLE: Thoreau in Walden states, "Our life is frittered away by detail."

RESEARCH PAPERS: Where footnotes are required, use the following example as a guide.

EXAMPLE: A great philosopher once said, "There is no cure for birth and death save to enjoy the interval."[1] A great naturalist stated that the mass of men lead lives of quiet desperation.[2] He went on to say, "I have traveled much in Concord."[3] Thoreau lived the philosopher's words, "It is wisdom to believe in the heart."[4]

SAMPLE FOOT-NOTES:

[1] George Santayana, Soliloquies in England (New York: Scribners, Inc., 1922), p. 41.
[2] Henry David Thoreau, "Economy," in Thoreau: Walden and Other Writings, ed. Joseph Wood Krutch (New York: Bantam Books, 1971), p. 111.
[3] Ibid., p. 108. [Ibid. means the same work, same title as in the footnote immediately preceding.]
[4] Santayana, op. cit., p. 49. [Op. cit. means "in the work cited" and refers to the title of a work used in a previous footnote, in this case footnote 1.]

For other footnoting, consult a standard guide to the research paper.

25 A

Footnoting and Bibliography

MECHANICS FOR BIBLIOGRAPHY

5 B **FOLLOW THE CONVENTIONS FOR THE MECHANICS IN SETTING UP THE BIBLIOGRAPHY.**

COMMENT: Always list alphabetically by author's last name.

EXAMPLE: *BOOKS*

Thoreau, Henry David, Thoreau: Walden and Other Writings. New York: Bantam Books, 1971.

MAGAZINES AND NEWSPAPERS

Burnham, Philip E., "The Legacy of Attalus." History Today, (May 1976), p. 310.

Reinhold, Robert, "New York Slows Population Loss." The New York Times, (July 4, 1976), p. 1.

ENCYCLOPEDIAS AND REFERENCE BOOKS

Dickens, Charles, The Oxford Companion to English Literature. New York: Oxford University Press, pp. 233-34.

BULLETINS

The Congressional Record. (March 19, 1976). Washington, D.C.: U.S. Government Printing Office, 1976, p. 36.

For other mechanics of bibliography, consult a standard guide to the research paper.

B 25

Appendix 1

SENTENCE

DEFINITION OF A SENTENCE

A *sentence* is a group of words (generally containing a subject and a verb) that expresses a *complete thought.*

NOTE: The *sentence* needs nothing added to it to convey its meaning to the reader.

The *subject* is the person, thing, or idea about which the sentence expresses a thought. It will always be a noun or pronoun.

The *verb* is a part of speech that acts for or upon the subject, or makes an assertion (predicates something) about the subject.

EXAMPLES OF SENTENCES: He hits the ball. (*He* is the subject; *hits* is the verb; *ball* completes the thought.)

Hit the ball. (Understood *you* is the subject; *hit* is the verb; *ball* completes the thought.)

EXAMPLES OF SENTENCE FRAGMENTS: When he hit the ball . . . (*He* is the subject, *hit* is the verb, but the thought is not completed. The reader says: "So what? Tell me more.")

He hit. (*He* is the subject; *hit* is the verb; the thought is perhaps *not* completed, depending on the context. The reader may still want to say: "Hit what? Tell me more.")

Appendix 1

SENTENCE

CLASSIFICATION OF SENTENCES ACCORDING TO TYPE

THE DECLARATIVE SENTENCE makes a statement (or denies it).

EXAMPLES: Chickens like to be fried.
Potatoes do not like to be fried.

THE INTERROGATIVE SENTENCE asks a question.

EXAMPLE: Do chickens like to lay eggs?

THE IMPERATIVE SENTENCE gives a command or makes a request.

EXAMPLES: Come here! Sit down. Listen carefully.

THE EXCLAMATORY SENTENCE expresses strong emotion.

EXAMPLES: How stupid he is! What a surprise!

CLASSIFICATION OF SENTENCES ACCORDING TO STRUCTURE

A SIMPLE SENTENCE has *one* subject and *one* verb.

EXAMPLE: School opened September 16.

(Continued on next page.)

Appendix 1

SENTENCE

A COMPOUND SENTENCE has *two or more independent* clauses.

EXAMPLE: School opened September 16, and everyone was happy.

A COMPLEX SENTENCE has *one independent* clause and *one or more subordinate* clauses.

EXAMPLE: When school opened September 16, everyone was jubilant.

A COMPOUND-COMPLEX SENTENCE has *two or more independent* clauses and *one or more subordinate* clauses.

EXAMPLE: The school, which opened September 16, had 750 students, and they were all happy.

(See Appendix 4, pp. 242-43, for *independent* and *subordinate* clauses.)

Appendix 2

PARTS OF SPEECH

THE *PART OF SPEECH* is a term used to designate a word's function or use. There are eight parts of speech.

Part of Speech	Use	Examples
1. Noun	Names a person, place, thing, state, quality, action	Tim, Greenwich, rat, wit, beauty, thinking
2. Pronoun	Takes the place of noun	he, they, we, who, what, this, one, somebody, that
3. Verb	Acts, links, expresses state-of-being	hit, walk, is, appear, seem
4. Adjective	Modifies nouns and pronouns	*strong* language She is *pretty*.
5. Adverb	Modifies verbs, adjectives, and other adverbs	hits *boldly* *rather* pretty *rather* prettily
6. Preposition	Relates a noun or pronoun with another noun, pronoun, or verb	Wizard *of* Oz two *of* us ran *to* the house
7. Conjunction	Joins words or groups of words	Bill *and* Mary He was here *when* I was.

(See 18A, 18B for coordinating and subordinating conjunctions.)

8. Interjection	Shows emotion	Oh! Hurrah! Bah! Humbug! Eh!

(Continued on next page.)

APP 2

Appendix 2

NOTE: When used as expletives, *it* and *there* are not parts of speech. They are devices used in English to help fill out the introduction of a sentence. They have no grammatical function.

EXAMPLES OF EXPLETIVES

THERE   *There* are many people here. (*People* is the subject. *There* weakly pads the introduction of the sentence. Expletives generally weaken the style by *pushing* the subject into the middle of the sentence.)

IT   *It* is stupid to steal. (Normal word order: To steal is stupid. *To steal* is the subject; *is* is the verb.)

THE USE OF THE WORD IN THE SENTENCE DETERMINES ITS PART OF SPEECH.

Consider *like* as a part of speech:
 We *like* candy. (Verb)
 Ray has a watch *like* mine. (Preposition)
 He believed in socialism and *like* ideas. (Adjective)
 He was subject to spells, fits, and the *like*. (Noun)

Consider *wrong* as a part of speech:
 A *wrong* does not make a right. (Noun)
 His answer is *wrong*. (Adjective)
 She did *wrong*. (Adverb)
 You *wrong* me by such accusations. (Verb)

Appendix 3

PHRASES

A PHRASE is a group of words containing neither subject nor verb. The phrase can be classified as noun, adjective, or adverb.

A PREPOSITIONAL PHRASE will always be introduced by a preposition and may be used only as an *adjective* or an *adverb*.

EXAMPLES: He lived *in a house.* (Adverb modifying the verb *lived.*)
The money *in my pocket* . . . (Adjective modifying the noun *money.*)

A VERBAL PHRASE is derived from a verb. It may be used as a noun, adjective, or adverb, and may take a direct object. There are three types of verbals.

Gerund: A gerund is a verbal used as a *noun* only.

A *gerund* has tenses and voice.

	Active	*Passive*
Present	hitting	being hit
Past	having hit	having been hit

EXAMPLES: He liked *hitting the ball.* (*Hitting the ball* is a gerund phrase in the present active, the object of the verb *liked.*)

He liked *being hit.* (*Being hit* is a gerund phrase in the present passive, the object of the verb *liked.*)

He liked *having hit the ball.* (*Having hit the ball* is in the past active, the object of the verb *liked.*)

He liked *having been hit by Dad.* (*Having been hit by Dad* is in the past passive, the object of the verb *liked.*)

(Continued on next page.)

APP 3

Appendix 3

PHRASES

Participle: A participle is a verbal used as an *adjective* only.

Like the gerund, a participle has tenses and voice.

	Active	*Passive*
Present	hitting	being hit
Past	having hit	hit, having been hit

EXAMPLES: We spotted Mary *hitting her brother.* (*Hitting her brother* is a participle phrase in the present active modifying *Mary.*)

We spotted her brother *being hit by Mary.* (*Being hit by Mary* is a participle phrase in the present passive modifying *brother.*)

We spotted Mary *having hit the ball.* (*Having hit the ball* is a participle phrase in the past active modifying *Mary.*)

We spotted the ball *hit* (or *having been hit*) *by Mary.* (*Hit* or *having been hit by Mary* is a participle phrase in the past active, modifying *ball.*)

Appendix 3

PHRASES

Infinitive: An infinitive is a verbal used as a *noun*, an *adjective*, or an *adverb*.

Like the gerund and participle, an infinitive has tenses and voice.

	Active	*Passive*
Present	to hit	to be hit
Past	to have hit	to have been hit

EXAMPLES: *To hit the ball* is fun. (*To hit* is an infinitive used as a noun, the subject of the verb *is.*)

He liked *to hit the ball*. (*To hit the ball* is an infinitive used as a noun, the direct object of *liked*.)

The man *to be hit* is Bill. (*To be hit* is an infinitive used as an adjective modifying the noun *man.*)

He put in a new pitcher *to save the game*. (*To save the game* is an infinitive used as an adverb modifying the verb *put.*)

NOTE: Almost invariably when the infinitive expresses purpose, (that is, answers the question "why?"), it modifies the verb in the main clause.

Appendix 4

CLAUSES

A *CLAUSE* (whether *independent* or *subordinate*) is a group of words that has a subject and a verb.

An *independent clause* is a sentence. It completes the thought. A *subordinate clause* is not a sentence. It cannot stand by itself.

Subordinate clauses have three different uses: nouns, adjectives, and adverbs.

NOUN CLAUSES function exactly like single nouns.

EXAMPLES: *That she is rich* is known to all of us. (*That . . . rich,* a noun clause, subject of verb *is known.*) We know *that she is rich.* (*that . . . rich,* a noun clause, object of verb *know.*)

We will give it to *whoever comes.* (*Whoever comes,* a noun clause, object of preposition *to.*)

ADJECTIVE CLAUSES are almost invariably relative clauses.

EXAMPLE: I know the girl *who came.* (*Who came,* a relative clause, used as adjective to modify noun *girl.*)

Appendix 4

SUBORDINATE CLAUSES

ADVERB CLAUSES function exactly like single adverbs.

EXAMPLES: She cried *because the cat was kicked.* (*Because . . . kicked,* adverb clause, modifies verb *cried.*)

He is stingier *than I am.* (*than I am,* adverb clause, modifies adjective *stingier.*)

He borrowed money more gracefully *than I did.* (*than I did,* adverb clause, modifies adverb *gracefully.*)

ELLIPTICAL CLAUSES have either subject or verb missing, but either can be supplied from context.

EXAMPLES: He needs psychotherapy more than I (need psychotherapy.)

While (I was) pondering my fate, I tripped over my cat.

Appendix 5

A CONCISE GUIDE TO WORD – USE – PART OF SPEECH

The examples in this appendix are provided as a concise guide to word – use – part of speech. Please follow the models *exactly*.

Use the following abbreviations:

adj. (adjective)

adv. (adverb)

app. (appositive)

cl. (clause)

conj. (conjunction)

coord. (coordinating)

D.O. (direct object)

expl. (expletive)

ger. (gerund)

I.O. (indirect object)

ind. (independent)

inf. (infinitive)

interj. (interjection)

introd. (introduces)

mod. (modifies)

n. (noun)

obj. (object)

o.p. (object of prep.)

part. (participle)

P.O.S. (part of speech)

phr. (phrase)

P.A. (pred. adj.)

P.N. (pred. noun or pred. nom.)

prep. (preposition)

pron. (pronoun)

RBT (refers back to and modifies)

s. (subject)

subord. (subordinating, subordinate)

v. (verb)

Appendix 5

A CONCISE GUIDE TO WORD – USE – PART OF SPEECH

Examples that follow demonstrate a precise method to indicate word, use, and part of speech.

EXAMPLE #1:   The parts of speech, and subject, verb, direct object, indirect object, object of preposition.

SENTENCE: A policeman in uniform kindly showed me his black pistol.

Word	Use	P.O.S.
A	mod. n. *policeman*	adj.
policeman	s. of v. *showed*	n.
in	introd. adj. phr.	prep.
uniform	o.p. *in*	n.
kindly	mod. v. *showed*	adv.
showed	v. of s. *policeman*	v.
me	I.O. of v. *showed*	pron.
his	mod. n. *pistol*	adj.
black	mod. n. *pistol*	adj.
pistol	D.O. of v. *showed*	n.

APP 5

Appendix 5

EXERCISE 1

DIRECTIONS: Following the method in this appendix, select the subjects, verbs, direct objects, indirect objects, and objects of prepositions, and give use and part of speech.

1. We generally gave the church and the state the savings of a lifetime.

2. Zina called her friend on Farmington Avenue.

3. Teachers seldom become millionaires.

4. Harriet always loved her animals but often forgot them.

5. Why did you send them gifts?

6. Tell your friends the truth, or they will hate you.

7. Julia's mother always makes her hamburgers.

8. The sinking boat foundered on the rocks.

9. The children disliked spinach, kidneys, and mushrooms.

10. Desmond entered the hospital for a minor operation.

11. Too many Canada geese made nests in our yard.

12. Under the bridge sailed the huge ocean liner.

13. During the summer, Mother sent me money and cookies.

14. Great Danes she disliked, but poodles she adored.

15. Elisabeth deeply enjoys reading and art.

Appendix 5

A CONCISE GUIDE TO WORD – USE – PART OF SPEECH

EXAMPLE #2:   Subject — linking verb — P.A. — P.N. — coord.
conjunction — interjection.

SENTENCE: Well, Jane is young, but she will become a woman.

Word	Use	P.O.S.
Well	exclamatory word	interj.
Jane	s. of v. *is*	n.
is	v. of s. *Jane*	v.
young	P.A. RBT. s. *Jane*	adj.
but	joins two cl. (coord.)	conj.
she	s. of v. *will become*	pron.
will become	v. of s. *she*	v.
a	mod. n. *woman*	adj..
woman	P.N. RBT. s. *she*	n.

APP 5

Appendix 5

EXERCISE 2

DIRECTIONS: Following the method in this appendix, select the subjects, verbs, predicate adjectives, predicate nouns, and
conjunctions, and give use and part of speech.

1. Bruce was a teacher, but his wife was a lawyer.

2. The flower was very beautiful but poisonous.

3. Truth is always a virtue.

4. The juicy steak on the fire smelled good.

5. The boys on the football team were happy but tired at the end
of the game.

6. In the cold breeze he always felt chilly and uncomfortable.

7. Were you the boy at the party?

8. Both she and Harry felt joyful after the party.

9. Candy or ice cream was her favorite treat.

10. Joseph eventually became a doctor.

11. Elisabeth is intelligent, artistic, and witty.

12. The sport of fishing was not Kristin's idea of an exciting
time.

13. The dessert was taken from the oven and looked sticky and
unappetizing.

14. Hoskins was a self-serving but independent man.

15. Neither Paula nor Chris seems upset at the prospect of losing.

Appendix 5

A CONCISE GUIDE TO WORD – USE – PART OF SPEECH

EXAMPLE #3:   Understood subject — expletive — prep. phrase.

SENTENCE: *Look* here! *There* is a *fly in my soup.*

Word	Use	P.O.S.
Look	v. of s.(You)	v.
There	expl.	–
is	v. of s. *fly*	v.
fly	s. of v. *is*	n.
in . . . soup	prep. phr. mod. v. *is*	adv.

EXAMPLE #4:   Verbals – appositive – subord. conjunction.

SENTENCE: *Although James, a boy* easily *discouraged,* liked *to play* hockey, he enjoyed *dancing* even more.

Word	Use	P.O.S.
Although	introd. adv. cl. (subord.)	conj.
boy	app. with *James*	n.
discouraged	part. mod. n. *boy*	adj.
to play	inf. D.O. of v. *liked*	n.
dancing	ger. D.O. of v. *enjoyed*	n.

Appendix 5

WORD — USE — PART OF SPEECH

EXERCISE 3. Prepositional phrases

DIRECTIONS: Following the method in this appendix, select the prepositional phrases in the sentences below, and give use and part of speech.

1. The man in the moon is a figment of your imagination.

2. During the course of his speech, Mr. Hockworth spoke in three languages.

3. Among the students were boys in white trousers.

4. The man with paint on his coat entered through the back door of the barn.

5. They drove to New York through the Lincoln Tunnel.

6. In the quiet of evening, they sat on the front porch of the house.

7. The teacher with Mary is the nastiest man at school.

8. Did the cat on the fence jump into the pool?

9. Beyond the hills stood the huts of the natives.

10. For dessert I was given a piece of cake with chocolate icing.

11. In the interest of brevity, Marc spoke for only five minutes.

12. They sailed across the bay with the sun at their backs.

13. The store on the corner is open every day from dawn until dusk.

Appendix 5

EXAMPLE #5:   Verbals (Other uses of infinitive – gerund – participle.)

SENTENCE: The *smiling* boy came *to say* that he had a right *to enjoy swimming.*

Word	Use	P.O.S.
smiling	part. mod. n. *boy*	adj.
to say	inf. mod. v. *came*	adv.
to enjoy	inf. mod. n. *right*	adj.
swimming	ger. D.O. of inf. *to enjoy*	n.

EXAMPLE #6:   Phrases (prepositional and verbal).

SENTENCE: *Wounded in the shoulder,* the captain *of the ship* asked *his aides to take him to the nearest hospital.*

Phrase	Use	P.O.S.
Wounded . . . shoulder	part. mod. n. *captain*	adj.
of . . . ship	prep. phr. mod. n. *captain*	adj.
*his . . . him	inf. phr. D.O. of v. *asked*	n.
to . . . hospital	prep. phr. mod. inf. *to take*	adv.

*(Some authorities consider this construction an infinitive clause with *aides* as subject and *to take* as a verb.)

251

APP 5

Appendix 5

A CONCISE GUIDE TO WORD – USE – PART OF SPEECH

EXAMPLE #7:   Clauses (Adjective – adverb – noun).

SENTENCE: *When he first entered school,* Jack, *who was quite intelligent,* thought *that teachers were ill-prepared.*

Clause	Use	P.O.S.
When. . . school	mod. v. *thought*	adv.
who . . . intelligent	mod. n. *Jack*	adj.
that . . . ill-prepared	D.O. of v. *thought*	n.

EXAMPLE #8:   Noun clauses (Subj. — P.N. — o.p.).

SENTENCE: *That you are stubborn* is *what I dislike,* but I do not know to *whom I will give this information.*

Clause	Use	P.O.S.
That . . . stubborn	s. of v. *is*	n.
what . . . dislike	P.N. RBT. *that* . . . *stubborn*	n.
whom . . . information	o.p. *to*	n.

Appendix 5

A CONCISE GUIDE TO WORD – USE – PART OF SPEECH

EXAMPLE #9:   Relative pronoun or subordinating conjunction.

SENTENCE: The members agreed *that* a new clubhouse was needed,

but the house *that* they wanted was too expensive.

Word	Use	P.O.S.
1 that	introd. n. cl. (subord. conj.)	conj.
2 that	introd. adj. cl. (rel. pron.)	pron.

EXAMPLE #10: Uses of *who* and *whom.*

Sentences	Word	Use	P.O.S.
Who are you?	who	s. of v. *are*	pron.
Whom did you ask for?	whom	o.p. *for*	pron.
Who did you think she was?	who	P.N. RBT s. *she*	pron.
He knew *who* it must have been.	who	s. of v. *must have been*	pron.

(In the sentence above, *it* is an expletive.)

It was Jack *whom* we saw.	whom	D.O. of v. *saw*	pron.

253

APP 5

Appendix 5

WORD – USE – PART OF SPEECH

EXERCISE 4. **Direct and indirect object — adjective — predicate noun — predicate adjective — expletive — preposition and object of preposition.**

DIRECTIONS: Following the method in this appendix, select the subjects and verbs and give use and part of speech. Also give use and part of speech of each of the italicized words.

1. A trip to a peanut *warehouse* can be an *enjoyable experience*.

2. My uncle *from* Chicago once bought *me* a *bicycle* with a five-speed *shift*.

3. Cara was *tall* and *attractive* but thoroughly *unpleasant*.

4. Will is a *man* of action and *adventure*, and he enjoys *movies* with *swordplay* and romance.

5. *There* are countless *atoms in* just one piece *of* matter.

6. Moira fed her *baby* a *mixture* of milk and *honey*.

7. Give *me* your *attention*, and you will learn some interesting *facts*.

8. Melanie has no *money* and will ask *Wilma* for a *dollar*.

9. *In* the distant future, man may be *happier* in outer *space* than *on* earth.

10. Neither Jason nor his parents are becoming *better at* skiing.

11. Muggsy's alibi seemed *unlikely*, and the police eventually arrested *him* for car *theft*.

12. Selma's Christmas gifts were a *violin*, a *zither*, and a *doll* with *bells*.

13. Cranston could not find the missing *jewels* and was a *failure* as a private *detective*.

14. Wilhelm's car is *bigger* than mine.

Appendix 5

WORD – USE – PART OF SPEECH

EXERCISE 5.   Includes all elements in Appendix 5.

DIRECTIONS: Following the method in this appendix, give use and part of speech of each of the italicized words in the sentences below.

1.   *There* is a true *story concerning* a man *who* bought a boat.

2.   He was a wealthy *man, but* he had *never* been in a boat.

3.   *When* he ordered a *motorboat* from the manufacturer, he specified *that* the cockpit of the craft be designed *like* the driver's seat of an automobile.

4.   The manufacturer, a *man who* never argued with the customer, designed the *boat* to the man's *specifications.*

5.   On the first trip, the *excited* man wanted *to test* the *speed* of the craft.

6.   *Knowing* his wife's *love* of speed, he asked *her to take* the controls.

7.   *Remarking* that she loved *boating,* the wife pushed the *accelerator* to the floor.

8.   The *stunned* observers on the dock watched *as* the boat sped in a wide circle in the harbor and quickly headed *back* to the pier.

9.   The *man's* wife reached for the brake *to slow* the boat, but of course *there* was no *brake.*

10.   With a *grinding* crash, the pier *and* the boat disintegrated.

APP 5

Appendix 5

WORD – USE – PART OF SPEECH

EXERCISE 6. Subordinate clauses.

DIRECTIONS: Following the method in this appendix, select subordinate clauses and give use and part of speech.

1. Although he is bright, Jim is a student who does not exert himself.

2. The teacher whom I asked to the party said that he could not come because his dog was sick.

3. When the moon rose, the vampire searched for victims that could supply him nourishment.

4. Dr. Kildare decided that an operation would be necessary if the patient became unruly.

5. After the baby had eaten the paint, I knew he would be sick.

6. The soldiers, who had marched all day, did not think that the enemy would attack during the night.

7. If parents think that teachers are human, they probably thin that children are human, too.

8. As the speaker was addressing the audience, a girl whom I knew began to scream.

9. Do you know who is going to the party after the dance is over ?

10. The book that he has is not the one that was taken from the library.

Appendix 6

A GUIDE TO EVALUATING YOUR COMPOSITION

Before writing a composition, you should be aware of the standards by which English teachers judge the content of a composition. These standards, of course, vary with individual teachers, and they — and only they — are the ultimate judges of the merit of your work.

However, there are certain guidelines that many teachers look for. The following items suggest some of these guidelines.

The Outline
1. Does the outline cover the subject?
2. Does the outline have overall organization?
3. Are the items phrased concretely?
4. Is the outline in proper topic form?

NOTE: (See Appendix 8 for the proper way to write an outline.)

Paragraphing
1. Does the opening paragraph of a *story* or *narrative* establish the setting? (Who? What? Where? When?)
2. Does the opening paragraph of a *description* or *essay* clearly state the purpose and arouse the reader's interest?
3. Does each paragraph have a topic sentence?
4. Does the paragraph stick to the subject?
5. Is there superfluous material in the paragraph?
6. Are specific, concrete examples used to illustrate the generalizations?
7. Are the paragraphs linked to one another?
8. Is the last paragraph an effective conclusion to the composition?

(Continued on next page.)

Appendix 6

A GUIDE TO EVALUATING YOUR COMPOSITION

Overall Organization

1. Are the ideas presented in a fresh and original manner?
2. Are the ideas presented clearly?
3. Has the writer used vivid, exact words and precise examples.
4. Has the writer established and kept to a point of view?
5. Is the composition free of unnecessary details?
6. Is the style consistent with the subject matter? (See 14I and 15F.)
7. Has the composition covered everything promised in the title or the opening paragraph?
8. Is there an overall unity to all the ideas?

Appendix 7

A SUGGESTED METHOD FOR WRITING A COMPOSITION

No set of rules will guarantee that the content of a composition will be successful. To paraphrase Thomas Edison, writing is 1% inspiration and 99% perspiration. In short, the more work (not necessarily *time*) you put into a composition, the better are its chances for success.

If your work has direction and discipline, the better the results are likely to be. This guide, then, is intended to aim your efforts in the right direction.

1. *Make sure you understand the topic.* Think about it in *concrete terms* and in terms of *design*. (What *specifically* do you want to say? Where do you want to begin? Where do you want to end?)

2. Jot down ideas as quickly as they occur. (See Appendix 8 — The Outline.)

3. Arrange these ideas in a logical outline. (See Appendix 8 — The Outline.)

4. Write your first copy *without interruption.* Let the words *flow freely.* Do not stop, for example, to look up a word in the dictionary. Underline or put an asterisk next to the word in question; look it up later (see step 6).

5. After completing the first copy of your composition, LET IT ALONE for a while. Do your Latin or mathematics, eat dinner. Then, with a fresh eye, return to your composition.

6. Now PROOFREAD and REVISE to correct grammar, punctuation, and spelling. Be alert for SENTENCE ERRORS and LAZY WORDS. Take out unnecessary words and details. In short, polish the prose to a high gloss.

7. Write your final copy neatly.

Appendix 8

HOW *NOT* TO WRITE AN OUTLINE

The outline can be extremely helpful in writing your composition. If done poorly, it can be no help at all.

Do *not* write an outline after you have written your composition. That's stupid.

Do *not* write and outline in vague, general terms.

Here is a model of an outline that does not help at all:

My Spring Vacation

I. Introduction (First paragraph *always* introduces subject)
   A. Getting ready (For what? Also, lazy word *get*)
   B. Making preparations (Same as IA. Why include?)
   C. We leave (Who is "we"? Leaving for where? Also, not parallel to IA and IB.)

II. Body (Says nothing)
   A. Where we went (Where *did* you go?)
   B. When we arrived (Give the time)
   C. What we did (What *did* you do? Say it)

III. Conclusion (Naturally!)
   A. We had fun (Why?)
   B. We pack up (Omit *up*. Is packing important?)
   C. We leave (See IC. You've left already)
   D. When we got home (Not parallel with IIIA, B, and C. Lazy word *got*. Is it important when you arrived home?)

Appendix 8

THE OUTLINE

HOW TO WRITE AN OUTLINE – STEP 1.

An outline is most helpful if you think in *concrete, specific* terms. Jot down as many vivid incidents as you can recall. At this point, there need be no organization to these incidents. Let the ideas come quickly.

My Spring Vacation

"What to pack?" said Mother
Buying airplane tickets
Father's impatience while packing
Taking off from Kennedy Airport
Bumpy landing at Nassau
The cute stewardess spills coffee on me
Swimming in crystal waters of Caribbean
Brightly colored fish
Superb food
The rain storm – spectacular
The beauty of the reef
The movie *The Birds* after dinner
Sister cuts foot on shell
Taking pictures
Return trip to Greenwich uneventful
Cold
Snowing
Depressing ride from airport to home
Depressing thought: school
Warm memories of Nassau
Unpacking suitcase
Ate dinner

Appendix 8

THE OUTLINE

THE OUTLINE – STEP 2.

If you are pressed for time, or even if you feel that you do not need it, you can afford to omit Step 1 on the previous page.

However, you *cannot* afford to omit Step 2. This step shapes the design, organization, and logic of your remarks.

Begin by setting up the three, four, or five major topics you wish to discuss, leaving blanks between them, in this manner:

My Spring Vacation

I. Frantic preparations for Nassau trip

II. Eventful flight to Nassau

III. Various activities at Nassau resort

IV. Depressing return to Greenwich

Appendix 8

THE OUTLINE

THE OUTLINE – STEP 3.

Finally, add specific, concrete examples to illustrate the main topics. (Use the items from Step 1, if you have made such a list.)

My Spring Vacation

I. Frantic preparations for Nassau trip
    A. Buying airline tickets
    B. Packing clothes
        1. Father's impatience
        2. Mother's indecision

II. Eventful flight to Nassau
    A. Takeoff from Kennedy Airport
    B. Coffee in my lap
    C. Bumpy landing at Nassau

III. Various activities at Nassau resort
    A. Swam in Caribbean
    B. Observed tropical fish
    C. Enjoyed superb food
    D. Watched tropical storm
        1. Clouds forming in west
        2. Whitecaps starting to form
    E. Took pictures
    F. Marveled at beauty of reef

IV. Depressing return to Greenwich
    A. Uneventful plane trip
    B. Miserable New York weather
    C. Warm vacation memories

Appendix 8

THE TOPIC OUTLINE – MECHANICS

Follow these rules in making an outline:

1. Place the title above the outline.

2. Do not use the terms *Introduction, Body, Conclusion.*

3. Use roman numerals for main topics.
   Use capital letters for subtopics.
   Use arabic numbers for sub-subtopics.
   Use small letters for sub-sub-subtopics.

   Proper arrangement of numbers and letters.

   I.
      A.
      B.
         1.
         2.
            a.
            b.

4. Indent subtopics so that like letters and numbers come directly under one another in a vertical line.

5. Begin each topic and subtopic with a capital letter.

6. Do not put a period at the end of topics.

7. Put at least two subtopics under each topic.

8. Use phrases – not sentences.

9. Make certain topics are grammatically parallel.
   Make certain all subtopics are grammatically parallel.

INDEX

References are to rule numbers except where otherwise specified (App., Chap., etc.). Numbers following references to appendixes and chapters refer to page numbers.

Indirect object,
case of, 10: 95, 10I, 10J
use of, 10: 95, 10I, 10J; App. 5: 245
Indirect statement
use *that*, 16B
Infer, imply, 14J
Infinitives
commas with, 2C
dangling, 20E
defined, 20D; App. 3: 241
parallelism of, 21: 216, 21A
phrase as sentence error, 1E
split, 20D
subject of, 10N
tense and voice, App. 3: 241
Informal words, 14D
In my opinion, I think,
abused, 15C
Interjections
commas with, 2D
defined, App. 2: 237
examples of, 2D
exclamation point with, 4E
Interrogative pronouns
cases with, 10E, 10O
declined, 10: 96
Interrogative sentence
defined, App. 1: 235
Interrupters
commas with, 2I
Into, in, 13I
Intransitive verb, defined, 12: 119
Intransitive/transitive,
confused, 12Q
Introductory clauses, phrases,
words, use of comma, 2B-2D
Irregular verbs, tabulation of, 12: 124
Is because, is when, like when, 13W
It, expletive,
avoid use of, 12P
defined, App. 2: 238
Italics, 6C
airplanes, 6C
foreign words, 6C
motion pictures, 6C
publications, 6C
ships, 6C
spacecraft, 6C
titles of books, 6C
trains, 6C
TV programs, 6C
words, numerals, 6C
letters referred to by
name, 6C

works of art, music, 6C
It's confused with *its,* 8H; 13X

J Jargon, avoid, 14I

K *Kid* (n.), for *child,* 14J
Kid (v.), for *tease,* 14J
Kind of, sort of, overused, 14J
Kind of a, sort of a
unnecessary *a,* 14J

L *Lay*
conjugation of, 12: 124
Lead, led
spelling of, 14J
Leap, principal parts, 14J
Leave, let
proper use of, 14J
Length of paragraphs, 23A
Letters of alphabet,
italics with, 6C
plurals of, 8I
Liable, likely,
see *Apt,* 14J
Lie, lay
do not confuse, 12S
principal parts, 12: 122; 12S
Like, for *as,* 13Q
Like when, avoid, 13W
Likely, liable
see *Apt,* 14J
Linking verbs
defined, 12: 119
list of, 12: 119
predicate adjective with,
13J
use, App. 2: 237; App. 5: 247
Logical ideas
lack of, 17A; 23B
-looking, avoid as type of suffix,
14J
Loose, stringy sentences, 13O; 22C
Lose, loose, 13X
Lots, lots of
for *much,* 13L

M *Mad* for *angry,* 14J
Made, made out, overused, 14J
Main clauses
see Clauses, independent
Make up, for *decide,* 14J
Malapropisms, 14H
Math for *mathematics,* 14J

270

271

273

274

275